Ralph A. Keifer

The Mass
in Time
of Doubt
The Meaning of the Mass
for Catholics Today

National Association of Pastoral Musicians
Washington, D.C.

CONTENTS

For George and Kathleen Stewart and all the members of the St. Giles Family Mass Community

A PERSONAL PROLOGUE

A couple of summers ago I spent several weeks in Papua New Guinea. While I was there I visited the war cemetery in Bomana, near the capital town of Port Moresby. I was deeply moved by the row upon row of graves of my father's generation, young Australian men between the ages of nineteen and thirty-one. Their British names recalled another cemetery a world away in a little East Anglian village, where my English father lies buried, killed at the age of twenty-five in a 1939 airplane crash. Not a dozen paces away from my father's grave stands a small monument to his best friend, who died in the same war, somewhere in Asia.

Standing in that tropical cemetery made me realize how small the world has grown, that twelve thousand miles from home I can touch such a vivid reminder of my origins. Papua New Guinea is no further in time from Chicago than Norwich Cathedral was for my Great Yarmouth ancestors. And I can reach Port Moresby from Chicago in less than a quarter of the time it would have taken my ancestors to travel from Great Yarmouth to London. Such is the power of modern technology. And such is its power, when harnessed to the unredeemed violence of the human spirit, that I can find the marks of a European war scarring a land of palm trees and onetime cannibals. Thanks to the combination of idiot accident, wondrous technology, and unspeakable violence, my world is utterly different from that of my father. As a result of these things, and the events that have unfolded in their wake, I no longer bear my father's family name, nor share his citizenship, nor belong to the church that baptized and buried him and our ancestors for sixteen generations before him.

In a world where the smoke of cooking fires rises through the roofs of thatched huts along with the sound of transistor radios, and where a war in the Orient can be watched from the comfort of our living rooms, we have all become neighbors to one another while yet strangers to our own past. If we have "lost a sense of the sacred," it is less because of what happens in church than because of what has happened to our world. If we are disoriented in prayer, well may we be. We have things to pray about that never touched our ancestors in their wildest dreams nor troubled their most terrible nightmares.

Everywhere I go, I find believers, or people who want to find a way to believe, saying that they would like somebody to "explain the mass" to them. In the deepest sense, it really cannot be explained, if it really is the mass. If it really is the body and blood of the Messiah, then there is always more to it than we shall find within the limits of our own little time and place in this world. But there is another sense in which explanation can and must be given. The mass must unfold for people in a way that touches their hearts and their lives. Otherwise, it will indeed be without meaning for them. All too often, explanations are given that are not explanations at all, because they are not faithful to the way people actually live and believe and experience the mass today.

I begin with a piece of my own story because it dramatizes what I think is the experience of all serious believers and would-be believers—that we live in a fractured relationship with our past, with our traditions, with our world. The mania for certainty and security—manifest in every pseudo-religious response from the flight into fundamentalism to the cult of the pope as a media personality—tells us how deeply all of us experience that fracture. Authentic prayer is scarcely possible today unless it is tempered by serious doubt. Honest church membership must accept dissent and disappointment as its companions. If we are to bring anything like our whole selves to the altar, we can scarcely leave these realities at the church door.

My effort, then, is to provide a responsible commentary for people who do, or wish they could, participate in the eucharist of the Catholic Church. The mass is not only a mystery. It is also prayer. And it is the ancient ritual of a large, old, and powerful institution. If it is prayer, then to understand it we must grapple with what it means to believe and pray in the world we live in. If it is the ritual of the institutional church, then we must also grapple with something of what it means to live with the church as it actually is.

Beyond that, the ancient ritual of the mass has recently undergone reform. Often enough, that reform has been implemented halfheartedly or ineptly. Where this happens, the mass is robbed of much of its power, beauty, and possibility. And so, serious commentary cannot simply gloss over the sad experience of ignorant or uncaring use of our ceremonies. The official mass book of the church, *The Roman Missal,* insists in its very first chapter that the mass is the action of the entire church. Thus responsibility for its decent celebration does not rest solely with the clergy. It is the right and the duty of the laity to protest ignorant or careless use of our ceremonies. In a word, responsible commentary demands that we acknowledge that doubt is part of believing, that dissent and disagreement is part of adult belonging, and that, often enough, more than bread is broken at our altars.

I would like to add a special word of thanks to Rev. Virgil Funk, president of the National Association of Pastoral Musicians, and to Daniel Connors, my editor at NPM.

I

PRAYER IN TODAY'S WORLD

No serious exploration of praying at mass can be done without first exploring the possibility of prayer today. The first question that normally occurs is not how to pray *at mass,* but how to pray *at all.* Unfortunately, we often block the exploration of the question by assuming that there *is* such a thing as private prayer, and by assuming, in fact, that private prayer is the starting point of *all* prayer. Beginning with the sense of not praying, we ask "How may I pray?" It may be more important to ask, "How do people pray?" especially in the context of biblical religion. No disciple asked Jesus, "How shall I pray?" They said instead and said together, "Lord, teach *us* to pray"—a fascinating request, in view of the fact that they asked the question after observing him go out alone to pray. And they received an equally fascinating reply—*"Our* Father . . ."—stressing the corporate and communal character of all prayer.

I do not mean to be so silly as to imply that people do not pray when they pray alone. Nor am I being so ridiculous as to insist that every kind of solitary prayer is somehow a miniature formal liturgy. I simply mean that prayer, as our mystical tradition knows very well, has some important parallels with sexuality. For instance, while there may be such a thing as solitary sex, there is no such thing as entirely private sex, at least not for anyone who is sane. The same is true of prayer. The very nature of prayer, like sexuality, has to do with relationship, with our place in the

1

world in relation to others. This is as true of the hermit in solitude as it is of the parishioner rising to sing a hymn with her family and neighbors. Even by keeping his distance, the hermit is marking out a certain kind of relationship to the rest of the world.

Also, contrary to the pious presuppositions of certain distorters of its message, the prayer of biblical religion is extremely worldly: it demands connection with this world and this life. The heart of the prayer of Jesus is "thy will be done on earth as it is in heaven." In fact, the New Testament scriptures portray Jesus in a radically *prophetic* role in this regard: He never prays except at table, or among his disciples, or in solitude where he grapples with issues of power and his mission (the desert, Gethsemane, his prayer in the night during his ministry). It is interesting that he never is portrayed as praying in temple or synagogue. We may certainly assume he did. But the portrayal of his prayer exclusively outside of those "churchy" settings doubtlessly underscores the relationship between prayer and mission in the world. For similar reasons, the New Testament authors, like the prophets before them, apply the language of cult and sacrifice only to the ordinary life of Christians in the world. For example, the Epistle to the Hebrews exhorts believers to worship God with reverence and awe. But it goes on in the next line to say, "Never cease to love your fellow Christians. Remember to show hospitality . . . " (Heb. 13:1-2). For biblical religion, worship is utterly inseparable from service of neighbor, and is authenticated only in what we would call the service of justice and peace. So vividly was this appreciated by the early Christians that they were put to death as atheists and subversives by those who thought religion should be a matter of the heart and not of public affairs, and that worship should be an event confined to the sacred space of sanctuaries.

It is this fundamental connection between prayer and the world that now precipitates a crisis of prayer. For if our world changes, the things we need to pray about will be different, too. In fact, if our world changes, we will undergo a profound crisis of faith. Philosophers and theologians may debate whether human nature always remains the same, or whether it changes through history. But one thing is certain. The human situation can change, and change dramatically. It must have so changed when our remote ancestors discovered fire, and it did again when they learned to store seeds and grow crops and domesticate animals. It changed once more when they discovered how to make metal tools. According to the Book of Genesis, this power over the world is part of humankind's being made in "the image and likeness" of God. And each time that that power is rediscovered afresh, the situation of humankind is revolutionized. Everything changes, from the kind of food that appears on the table, to the shape of family living, to the kind of work that is done, to the forms of government, and to the kind of religion that people find best responds to their hopes, fears, trials, and triumphs. When the human situation changes, the image of God changes, too.

Within the very lifetime of many of us, humankind has passed through one of those crucibles of human experience that has changed the human situation as surely and completely as did the discovery of fire, the invention of planting and harvesting, the domestication of animals, or the use of metals. We humans have found ourselves able to do things we could never do before. In the span of a single generation, we have invented and used the Bomb, perfected the Pill, and walked on the moon. Within that generation we have obeyed the command of Genesis to increase, multiply, fill the earth and subdue it. We have obeyed it so fully that our very survival as a race depends on cutting back population growth and reversing the savaging of the earth. In the same generation, we have failed all faith, humanity, and sense by the slaughter of the gentle Jews of Germany and Eastern Europe. For the first time in human history, the human race is potentially no longer confined to this planet. Conversely, it is potentially capable of its own genocide in nuclear holocaust. Humankind, as never before, is lord of life and death. The decision for childbearing is ours, and if the race undergoes destruction, it will be at its own hand.

Never before in its history has the human race held such power and responsibility in its hands. At the same time, never before has it known such helplessness. Two thousand years of Christianity did not save Europe from the worst war the world has ever known. For all the wonders of our technology, with their ability to rescue us from drudgery, with their showering us with

3

a thousand comforts, with their amazing power to heal, save, and prolong life, we are unable to stop fouling our own nests with the pollution of earth, air, and water. The very rivers and seas stand close to being but the sewers and cesspools of humanity. For all the marvels of modern communication, when the voice of any other human being on earth is but the lifting of a receiver away, and where it is possible to go anywhere within a day's travel, our diplomacy perpetually hangs on the edge of wars that could end all life on the planet. For all the entanglements of multinational corporations and conglomerates webbing the globe, we are unable to develop any sort of constructive and cooperative plan to assure the equitable distribution of wealth and a general sense of participation in developing the world's welfare. Our children can tour Paris before they are out of their teens, yet suburban parents eat their hearts out over whether they are instilling sufficient "discipline" in them. National policy can send men to the moon and rockets to the stars, but it can find no constructive way to contain chronic unemployment or improve the education of the children of the poor.

And there is no way back. Once a technological change has begun to revolutionize a culture, the change is permanent and irreversible. A simple example will suffice. It takes about four days to cut down a tree with a stone axe. Introduce the steel axe into a culture that has some investment in cutting down trees, and you will irreversibly change the culture. For if it begins to take only an hour to cut down a tree, then the treecutter will begin to find other ways of filling the rest of the four days. The whole pattern of life will change. Within a generation, it will change irreversibly and totally, for the art of making stone axes will have been forgotten, and the bonds and alliances necessary with the suppliers of steel axes will have taken the place of the old ways. People will find their lives populated by new neighbors and their days filled with new ways. There will be no way back.

If such people are at all religious, the advent of the steel axe will obviously give them different things to pray about. And if the stone axe has been associated with the most important sources of life and power, its passing may well precipitate a profound crisis of faith. Someone speaking of nineteenth century French

4

peasants arriving in Paris to begin a new city life said that you could see them losing their faith as they crossed the railroad station. Of course. If religion was seen as totally bound up with peasant life, then its connection with the new life of the city was not easy to grasp.

It is the new social, political, and economic conditions ushered in by the new technology that call for new images of God. Because of the legal separation of church and state, we Americans are prone to assume that religion and politics have nothing to do with one another. Likewise, because we were so vigorously catechized to think of religion as dealing with our "souls," we sometimes tend to discount the religious impact of society and economics— areas that seem more related to the body. And because we take our working vocabulary about God mostly (whether directly or indirectly) from the Bible and the liturgy, we assume that religious language has some special sacred source outside the patterns of ordinary human life. But this country's easy association of flag and altar should be a signal that, in reality, sacred and secular are interwoven far more than we realize. This is nothing new. The language of our favorite divine titles (Lord, Almighty, Most High, etc.) is in fact the same language that was used in the courts of kings. So also the traditional images of the action of God are political ("Thy kingdom come," etc.). This use of the "profane" as image of God and his work in the world is not confined to language about God, either. Words like bishop (overseer), priest (from presbyter, senior citizen, council member), diocese (similar to the American state), are all derived from secular use. The traditional titles of the pope, religious as they sound (e.g., Servant of the Servants of God, Supreme Pontiff), were in fact originally the titles of the Roman emperor. Even our supposedly sacred vesture is simply a stylized and decorated inheritance from the garb of Roman officials, just as the use of lights, incense, water and processions in church ceremonials derives from the usages of the Roman imperial court. Again, this is nothing new. The language of the psalms was filled with the images of the political, social, and economic life of ancient Israel. The Latin word *commercium,* from which our word *commerce* derives, is a fascinating example of the combining of ordinary life and religion, which

5

is basic to authentic prayer language. Depending on the context, *commercium* stood for "nuptials,"[1] for the nature of the relationship between God and the world and Christ and his church, and for the sacred action of the eucharist.

And so, a changing world provokes a crisis of religious language. When our world changes, we are at a loss as to how to address God because the old images no longer work. God, to be God at all for us, is at the same time *strange* and *mysteriously present*. That strangeness is normally signaled by the use of all sorts of archaic images. Urban folk, for example, sing about unknown things like shepherds and the desert. Or people in democratic societies carry on in prayer in a language of king, throne, and scepter. But for the archaic image to "work," it must also be joined to something fresh and familiar; otherwise God cannot be experienced as present. The twenty-third psalm is a perennial favorite because it combines two things—the imagery of shepherds and pastures, which is foreign to the majority of believers, and a more subtle imagery of mothering care, which every whole human being has known.

The problem is that our world has changed so much that perhaps most of our religious language is rendered strange, without sufficient connection with the familiar and everyday to give it strength and substance. Signals of this crisis of language abound. It has certainly been at work in the preoccupation with liturgical reform that has swept over all the major churches. If some people experience liturgical reform as turning everything inside out and upside down, their perception is not at all inaccurate. For the attempt of liturgical reform is, on the one hand, to return to the sources of tradition, plumb the depths of the past, and restore old forms to a new vigor. On the other hand, it is also an attempt to join the old and restored with the fresh and the new, linking precisely the very strange and the very familiar. The Constitution on the Liturgy of Vatican II carefully stated exactly that goal: "Mother Church desires to undertake with great care a general restoration of the liturgy itself . . . .

---

[1] I don't use the term to be quaint. It is the only one we have to say "the wedding and everything else it implies."

The Christian people, as far as is possible, should be able to understand . . . with ease." And so, in large measure, what was done was to restore many things that had disappeared (e.g., the prayer of the faithful at mass), while introducing the vernacular language. We may ask some questions—and will, in this book—about that reform's effectiveness, but the effort at reform reflects a serious grasp of the issue.

The effort to "go back," to "restore" the old, is a clear symptom of our crisis of religious language. Efforts have not been limited to those of the official church. On the conservative side, charismatic renewal returns to speaking in tongues and an effort to reappropriate the language of the New Testament, while Archbishop Lefebvre and his followers cling fiercely to the old Latin Mass. On the radical side, probings of the cults of the mother goddess and witchcraft reflect an effort to get beyond Christianity and its perceived limits. The surest sign of crisis is the felt need to create a universe of God-talk, even if that universe be ever so small—a need of many of the groups I have just mentioned.

Having said that religious language, at least in biblical religion, is inevitably a language about this world as well, it is now possible to explore some of the reasons why we find ourselves alternately mute before a silent God or speechless with righteous and rightful rage before a cruel one, and why flight into fundamentalism or nostalgia or angry abandonment of the tradition altogether is often preferable to facing that awful void where the face of God has been eclipsed. The horrible problem for the believer, as we shall see, is that there is not even a clean void. To keep on believing requires not only that we take the courage to stand in the void, but also that we learn the patience to live with the debris of all the unlivable images of God that have littered down around us.

Except for the mystical or philosophical few, God is never God in Godself, but the God of ourselves and our world. Biblical religion comes down thoroughly on the side of God as One related to us and to our world. God is the God of Israel, the God of Abraham, the God of Isaac, and the God of Jacob; and Jesus names that God as our Father. The very names of Jesus Christ

7

(meaning savior, messiah or anointed one, king) are not the names of some metaphysical Second Person of the Trinity, but of One in relationship to *us*. A savior implies someone saved, and a messiah has to have people to be messiah for. You can't be a savior without the saved or a king without subjects any more than you can be a husband without a wife, or a sister without a sibling And therein lies the problem. If God is related to the world, then a change in *our* relationship to the world necessarily affects our relating to God. We need then, first, to explore something of the ways in which the Bomb, the Pill, the Computer, the Holocaust, and the Moon Walk have changed our relationship to the world.

Our Relationship to the Cosmos

In becoming capable of determining when life shall begin and end on this planet, as well as becoming able to walk on the moon, our race fully enters a phase that first dawned on it when Copernicus theorized that the earth revolves around the sun rather than vice versa. That Galileo should have been tried for heresy for defending Copernicus' theory is not surprising. As we now know very well, the world becomes a very different place when we no longer think of the universe as centered in the planet earth. We have so long been accustomed to accepting Copernicus' and Galileo's view of things, however, that we forget what the old theories *meant* when they were in full vigor.

For roughly two thousand years before Copernicus, people thought of the earth as the center of the universe. But the important thing was that they also had other thoughts that went along with that view of the place of the earth. They were aware that the moon revolves around the earth, as they were aware that the planets also move about. So they saw the universe as successive concentric spheres, with the earth in the center, the moon in the sphere above it, wandering planets beyond the moon, the moving sun beyond the moon, and, beyond that, the fixed stars. The closer you came to the earth, the closer you came to the sphere of change and decay, and the further away you got from it, the

8

more you entered into spheres of fixity, permanence, and most important, perfection. Greek thought located God, of course, in the outermost sphere.

For those who took this cosmology seriously, the whole business of religion as relating people to God suffered some serious difficulties. To get to God involved getting out of this world, and involvement with things that touched change or decay in any way was a clear sign of noninvolvement with God. It created a climate where it seemed normal that there should be an elite ascetical few who were capable of seeking God seriously, while the rest could be left to the messy pursuits of this world.

That view of things drew some especially negative marks for sexuality in general, and women in particular. Sex, involved as it is with the body, change, and generation, was easily viewed as at best a necessary evil. Women, as "obviously" under the influence of lower bodies such as the moon, with their monthly rhythm, could be seen as especially subject to the lower powers of the universe, and, therefore, as "obviously" inferior. The impact of these sorts of attitudes on Christianity, especially Catholic Christianity, scarcely needs commentary. Most of them are still with us, especially in the practices and statements of the official church, and most especially in the shape of its rituals. The exaggerated reverence with which we handle materials in worship—more concerned with people spilling the chalice or dropping a crumb from the host, than with people appreciating that the sharing of a meal together is *the* ultimate sign of what God's kingdom looks like—is the direct result of this sort of thinking, as is the preoccupation with priestly and institutional power, prerogatives, titles, insignia, and status. If we assume that God is somehow outside the world, beyond the world, then there must be superspecial vehicles by which he may be brought into the world. Deeply influenced by a cosmology that stressed the apartness of God from the world, the church cultivated apartness as the sign of sanctity. This is why most of the lives of the saints have become unreadable. Their major preoccupation is with the peculiarities of the saints and their extraordinary feats.

Now that human beings have jumped around on the moon and left their litter there, there can be no question of looking at the

9

stars and thinking of them as "heavenly bodies" in the way our ancestors did. We know that there is no successively more sacred ring of spheres out there, but only more of the same. If God is to be found, it cannot be somewhere "out there." If we are to find God anywhere it will have to be within the world.

Our Relationship to the World

The cosmos, I have suggested, gives God a face. How we think of the shape of the cosmos deeply affects how we think of God, and especially how we conceive God to be present in the world. But people do not simply see themselves as "in" the world. They act upon it and toward it. At the dawn of humanity, people seem to have been more preoccupied with gathering food than with contemplating the sunrise. Childbirth was doubtless given more sustained and regular attention than cave painting. And the Neanderthals, who left no monuments to their great ones, have left us the remarkable record that they celebrated funerals: their graves are filled with spores of pollen from the beds of flowers on which they buried their dead. At its barest minimum, human life requires that food be found or given, and no other creatures share food as we do. Likewise, the attention of all human beings must be drawn to our death and our sexuality—to the one, because we alone among the creatures know we must die, and to the other, because of the inherent paradox that we are all of a determinate sex, yet that the human race is irrevocably divided into two different kinds of human beings. We are the same as all living things in that we must eat, give life, and die, but utterly different in the way we know it and do it together. By our power, then, and our sexuality, and our death, we are both united to nature and divided from it, at home in the world yet pilgrims on the face of the earth. And in, with, and through these three central human preoccupations, rise the major concerns of religion. The language of prayer is a language of and about power, sexuality, and death.

This gives some ready clues to the problem of prayer today. If a God somewhere "out there," apart from the world, is no longer emotionally tenable, there is also difficulty locating God in this world, especially the God of biblical religion, whom the whole tradition presents as singularly preoccupied with morality. The God of the Bible takes Israel into the desert and draws her into covenant with some very specific instructions as to the kinds of behavior that are characteristic of those who relate to that very involved and concerned God. The kind of religion that provides a certain sacred dimension to the basic events of birth, marriage, and death, that provides comforting rituals in time of trial, and that legitimates the conventional morality of what is taken to be the proper behavior of "good citizens," has been with the human race since the very beginning.

People may, of course, and still do, use the Christian churches in this fashion—having their babies dutifully "done," showing up for weddings and funerals, or even fairly regularly attending because it is good "discipline." This may be a good thing, and it may even be prayer, but there is nothing especially biblical or Christian about such practice unless it is animated by the Spirit of Israel's God and his Christ, who has long insisted that humankind does not religiously live by bread alone, even the bread that churches provide. In commentary on Jesus' summation of the whole law and the prophets in the commands to love God and neighbor, it must be said at the very least that, according to biblical religion, human power and sexuality are always to be subordinated to the good of all, and that the demands of justice are to supersede our whims and wants.

Biblical faith, then, prays to love justice and to do the works of peace above all other petitions ("thy kingdom come," "thy will be done"). The thanksgiving of biblical prayer reaches beyond thanks for the beauty of nature or for what people today would call luck, and reaches to thanksgiving for God having so privileged the race with such a calling ("Our Father who art in heaven, hallowed be thy name"). And biblical prayer finds room for repentance, not simply because conventions have been broken or taboos outraged, and certainly not simply to relieve the threat of divine wrath, but because justice and peace have not been served and reconciliation is now sought ("forgive us our trespasses as we forgive those who trespass against us"). And in all of this, the bottom line is that we are called to prefer that thirst for justice and peace even to life itself. Obedience, even to death on the cross, is what marks the faithful one. "Lead us not into temptation but deliver us from evil" is not a prayer for rescue from all harm, but a prayer to stand firm in the face of harm.

The trouble is that when the sources of power and sexuality become enmeshed in a previously unknown technology, then what constitutes the work of justice and peace, or what constitutes the loving thing, is much more difficult to determine. The Pill, for instance, creates a new sexual universe because it inevitably unties reproduction from sexual expression. The traditional protest that it is "unnatural" scarcely remains credible in a world entirely enmeshed in technology. The very media by which Catholics know that the pope is against birth control are part of that wedding with artificiality which is the warp and woof of modern life. With the full arrival of modern medicine, the decisions as to who shall be born, and when, and who shall die, and when, are decisions more and more in human hands. Whether one is for or against birth control or abortion is rather beside the point. Wherever one stands or has stood, the field bristles with questions never before asked or askable.

This is as true of the "liberal" issues of social justice and world peace as it is of the "conservative" issues of birth control and abortion. As anyone knows who goes deeper than signing a petition or joining a march, the concrete steps toward justice and peace can only be taken within the sources of power—government, business, and industry—and that involves situations fraught with thickets of ambiguity, where every piece of moral progress will involve some sort of compromise.

The very experience of power has shifted radically. On the one hand, the race as a whole enjoys more power than it ever did: it can explode the atomic bomb and fly to the moon. On the other hand, the individual feels less powerful than ever before. Suburban executives feel as "caught" in their world as ghetto gang members in theirs. Scarcely a century ago, the majority of the population lived on subsistence farms, while today, the majority in this country are city dwellers. The subsistence farmer might be at the mercy of wind, weather, and soil, but the same farmer saw the fruit of his own toil and skill before his own eyes, and the small things of life were in his control. He and his wife not only raised their own food, but also fixed their own tools and built their own house. The human world around was a world they themselves had created. Today, the price of the complex technologies that sustain us is that no single individual has control over them. With the advent of the electronic watch, you are no longer in a position even to fix your own watch!

And so, it is not so clear as it once was (from the perspective of the doer) whether one has done justice and pursued peace. It is not so easy to rejoice over moral achievement, as equally it is not so easy to determine moral failure. For a religion whose God is preoccupied with ethics, this terrible ambiguity often deprives the believer of either the pride of belonging to the family of the faithful, or the joy of returning home in repentance. It should be no surprise that we have difficulty getting Lent off the ground, and that people have deserted the confessional in droves, just as it should be no surprise that a real sense of festivity is often difficult to come by. These things are all obscured by a cloud of ambiguity.

The Relationship to History

This ambiguity with which we now live readily leads to a sense of being betrayed by one's tradition. It is not simply that the church thunders prescriptions over moral minutiae (e.g., by preferring one technology of birth control over all others) while sounding an extremely uncertain trumpet over the matters that will determine the future of the very survival of the race (e.g., by having no clear direction to its stand on warfare or the nuclear arms race). Close to home is the fact that its collective and historical wisdom generally fails to be enough for the times in which we live. This is doubtless one of the major reasons for the widening rift between the teachings of Catholic theologians and the pronouncements of bishops and popes. We have run out of steam on the specialty that worked best for us—the wisdom of the ages.

13

But the ages never saw the Bomb or the Pill or the Moon Walk. They also never saw the Holocaust of European Jewry. Most of us Christians and Catholics are too readily inclined to ignore the Holocaust. But it was *the* religious event of our time. For Jews, who take it seriously, the Holocaust changes the whole of their history, because it represents God's breaking of the covenant with his people. Such manifest innocence went to its death, such unspeakable atrocity was perpetrated upon these men, women and children, that it is no longer possible to use the traditional explanations of persecution that absolved God of complicity. This means that all of Jewish history must be seen from a new and terrible angle.

For Christians, more is ultimately at stake than asking the questions that need to be asked about the anti-Jewishness[2] of much of the Christian tradition, including its gospels. This is an important starting point, but it is scarcely enough. The greater number of Jews went to their deaths in the midst of Christian, and in most cases, Catholic populations. In fact, the greatest number annihilated were from Catholic Poland, three million Jews from the midst of a nation more than nominally Catholic, supposedly in fact a "strong" Catholic nation. The handful of Catholic hands and voices raised against this unspeakable atrocity is not sufficient to put down the question which must be asked. Whatever may be said about the complicity of Pius XII, and certainly he was no heroic voice against the Nazis, the ordinary practicing Catholics of Germany and eastern Europe had a hand in the Holocaust of European Jewry.

Where, then, was the promise "I am with you always, even unto the consummation of the world"? Where, then, was the power against which it was promised that the gates of hell would not prevail? The Holocaust is not simply *the* moral atrocity of our age. It lays a shadow of doubt against the Christian message itself, for where, in that dark day, was the promised Holy Spirit of the last times? Even more, there has not been a word or tear

---

[2]Why do we always refuse to acknowledge the hate by masking anti-Jewishness with the vague term antisemitism?

of public repentance for this horror. The Declaration on Non-Christian Religions of Vatican II does not even mention the Holocaust, and upon the pope's visit to Auschwitz he chose to praise the handful of Catholic martyrs, while not even mentioning the Jews at all by name. The Holocaust puts hard questions to a people who worship the sacramental flesh and blood of the Messiah, while silently conniving in consigning his physical and historical flesh and blood to the ovens.

This is not to suggest any superiority of Catholics on this side of the Atlantic in this generation, but simply to observe that the event challenges us especially because there is nothing to prevent its happening again. Both Jew and Christian must grapple with the failure of what have been known as God's promises. For the Jew, the mystery of the delay of the Messiah remains. For the Christian, the delay of the kingdom ushered in by the Messiah is no less an enigma. In either case, the grounds for trust in God are shaken.

Our Fractured Relationship with the Sacred

The problem of prayer, then, is not simply a private problem. It is a problem of culture, a culture that has rapidly developed a new kind of technology, unleashing terrible new forces for evil as well as incredible power for good, and where the biblical tradition, if it is to find any sort of adequate answers, can no longer afford (if it ever could) to look mainly to the collective wisdom of its inherited past. Ultimately, we will have to write a third testament to be adequate to the religious situation of our time. The "loss of the sense of the sacred" is rooted less in the rather modest change of ceremonial we have undergone, than in the change of our situation in the world. In a cosmos endlessly littered with hunks of inert rock and potentially cluttered with the debris of human exploration, God can no longer be conceived of as "out there" for the simple reason that there is no longer any "out there." As the planet Earth has become one world of people, so also the cosmos has become one world with the planet. There may be more of it, but moon rock is just plain rock. Of course, anyone whose faith had matured beyond the point of being able to distinguish between believing in Santa Claus and believing in God has known for a long time that God is not literally "out there." It did not take a moon walk for believers to grasp that. But that is not the point. The point is, the religious *imagination* is deeply affected now that we have fully tasted what it means to live in a cosmos where the earth is not even the center of the solar system, and is in fact one floating speck among countless billions of others.

Of course, we can still "make pictures in our heads" of God being somehow "out there." But our hearts are not engaged in the same way as our ancestors' were with the pre-Copernican view of the universe. The real point is this: that as long as we were able to locate ourselves imaginatively at a fixed point in the universe, we could also "locate" God, and have a sense of God as "placed." And so God was comfortably and clearly located for believers in heaven, or in the voice of God's authorities on earth—clergy and scriptures—or in certain specific actions—especially, obviously, sacred rituals. If we were to think of God acting in the world, it was to think of God as acting like an invader from outside, operating on the world much as a little girl works with her dollhouse. And once we lose our sense of inhabiting a fixed place in space, the locating of God becomes a problem. And if church life and ritual lie under question, it is because its language, life, and ritual are all derived from the time when people could still imaginatively locate themselves in a fixed place in the cosmos.

It is true, of course, that some believers are still able to inhabit a pre-Copernican universe of thought, prayer, and activity, at least to some extent. I recently read, for instance, about a prominent priest who spends his Christmases in Latin America, among the poor, so he can celebrate mass with them. He said that he finds it worth spending his Christmases away from home so that he can "bring Jesus" to these people who would not otherwise have him. We may well applaud both the sacrifice and the deep faith which this generous act involves. But we may equally well question the description of the holy eucharist as the making present of an absent Jesus. Such a description is only adequate to a world where God can be imagined as somehow "out there."[3]

The disquiet that attends the inability to "locate" God is compounded by the experience of moral ambiguity now inherent in any effort to live a principled life in our complex world. The biblical tradition affirms a personal God. Contrary to popular notions of what that means, it does not mean primarily that the believer is expected to be able to directly experience God as One who is somehow like other human persons we know and love. Even the mystics who use the language of intimacy to describe their encounters with God insist that their language is utterly inadequate to the reality, only a pale analogy of the real thing. To say that God is "personal," then, is not to affirm that God is somehow like human persons, much less that we should enjoy some sort of experience of God as if God were a human person whom we intimately know. Some people's imaginations may be capable of conjuring up such experience, as some sorts of devotional patterns in the past were able to sustain it. But the tradition's experts in prayer are also unanimous in dismissing such experience as that of mere beginners in the spiritual life.

What it means to say that God is personal is that God is related to our lives and has a claim on us, a claim perceived as a blessing, and for which the believer rejoices, as well as praying that it continue, and, when the believer fails, praying to live again in faithfulness to that claim. For Christians, that is what it means to pray "through Christ our Lord," It does not mean that the believer feels Christ present at her side, or imagines that Christ stands before some throne pleading for the believer. Rather, it simply means that the believer is willing to put her life on the line, that with Christ our Lord she is willing to go to death (or live life unto death, which may be more difficult), to be an agent of justice and peace in the world.

---

[3]While piety has given every impression that a Catholic understanding of the eucharistic presence of Christ locates him in a place, and while one would certainly gain that impression from our rituals and church furnishings, the doctrine of the Catholic Church, interestingly enough, explicitly denies that Christ is contained in the eucharistic bread and wine as if he were located in a place. The official doctrine of transubstantiation excludes such a possibility. See the Summa Theologica of Thomas Aquinas, Pt. III, Q. 76, art. 5&6.

And finally, added to the inability to locate God in the cosmos, or to find God's claim clearly in the projects of our lives, there is the dark horizon of the violence of Christian history. The church (and not simply its hierarchy, or its official teaching, or its rituals and sacraments, but the whole church, including its people) has been traditionally known as a place of saving grace. For centuries, indeed, we taught that "outside the church there is no salvation." Yet in the very year when the pope produced an encyclical reaffirming the nature of the church as the mystical body of Christ, Hitler's Final Solution was applied, and the first members of Christ's historical flesh and blood were being sent to the ovens. Worse, while the blood of our Christ was being let in the German camps, the German bishops were busy being shocked by people who thought the laity should drink from the chalice. Against that obscene horizon, Christianity is a religion of broken promises. For if the present experience of the cosmos and of the world lays questions against the church, the experience of the church in history lays questions against God and his Christ.

Toward a Spirituality of Mystery

What, then, is the possibility of prayer today? In a less terrible age, John Henry Newman said that ten thousand difficulties do not make a single doubt. Today, it may be more appropriate to observe that ten thousand doubts do not add up to an ultimate difficulty against prayer. Biblical religion has no ultimate problem with doubting God and putting God to the question. Job and the psalms of lament are proof against that, as are the lives of the prophets. The Gospel according to John, which suppresses at almost every turn any serious portrayal of Jesus as an ordinary human being, balks at denying that humanity when it comes to the prayer of Jesus. So we find Jesus weeping at the tomb of his friend Lazarus, and facing his own death with that anguished cry, "My God, my God, why have you forsaken me?" One could name any number of saints whose prayer was attended by radical doubt, including one whose refreshing honesty has been virtually buried under the pastel petals of sentimental piety—Thérèse

18

of Lisieux. But it has been our sister faith, Judaism, that has more readily questioned God than we have, and perhaps the time has come to learn from her. During most of its history, Christianity has been "on the way up," a religion succeeding socially, politically, and culturally. At the same time, Judaism was constantly confined and persecuted. Our willingness to suppress doubt, and Judaism's willingness to express it, may have had something to do with that situation. In a world where the triumph of Christianity is not an assured or even necessarily a desired outcome, we may well have much to learn from a tradition more accustomed to disestablishment and disenfranchisement.

We may also note the strange paradox that attends the present situation. The cry of protest against the silence of God is in fact a reverberating echo of the message the biblical tradition identifies as the voice of God in the first place. If we suffer anguish because we can no longer locate God in the world, who taught us to expect to find God there? If the ultimate moral outrage is the difficulty of knowing when we have done the moral thing, who put this passion for true justice in our hearts? If we must protest that God has not kept his promises, who filled us with the expectation that God is to be trusted? If the church fails us and disappoints us, and we are shocked by the disparity between its sacraments and its politics as we are disgusted by its inversion of priorities, whence the hope for a more heavenly Jerusalem, and from where do we derive this vision of a people redeemed? "Your longing is your prayer," St. Augustine once observed, "and if your longing is continual, then you pray always." The God of biblical religion is a God of history, a God of people, and a God with a voice. In these voices, outside ourselves and within us, we may discern the life in the present silence of God. At what we used to call the Last Gospel, at the end of mass, we genuflected at the words in the prologue to the Gospel of John, "The Word was made flesh and dwelt among us." In this outrage against outrage, this hope against all hope, we may discern the echo of that Word for our own time. There can be no other way of finding God except within the world, no way of finding God's answer except within our own questions.

One of the most unhelpful things we have ever done is to take a one-on-one conversation as our model for prayer. This is, of course, based on the faulty assumption that God is "personal" in the same way human beings are "personal." It is also based on serious misreadings of scripture, which never holds this up as an exclusive model. Most of the prayers that, at first sight, look like one-on-one conversational pieces with a direct address to God, turn out to be prayers for use in a public ritual setting (like many of the thanksgiving psalms), or summaries of attitudes (like the Lord's Prayer, which is really not a prayer but is instead a catechism of what it means to pray). Most of the prayers which speak most intimately of God speak in the third person— God did this, God did that. It should be of some interest that in the biblical portrayal of Mary, whom Catholic piety has made the supreme model of prayer next to Christ himself, Mary addresses not a word of her prayer to God. Her *Magnificat* is a response to Elizabeth, not directly addressed to God!

Where we are given portrayals of people actually engaged seriously in the business of prayer, the heart of the matter is neither praise nor petition, but obedience. Not, of course, the childish yet demonically naive "blind obedience," which is a sick parody of the obedience even unto death on the cross, but the obedience of those who wrestle with living the mission they sense has been laid upon them. Abraham and the sacrifice of Isaac, Moses before the burning bush, Solomon and Isaiah in the temple, Jesus in the desert and at Gethsemane, and Mary questioning the angel even as she trembles—these are among the biblical models of prayer. If intimacy is involved, it is not the intimacy of friends, lovers, and companions, but the terrible intimacy of being given a task that the bearers sense will shape their whole life and demand the attention of their whole heart, without them wholly wishing it could be that way, and without them having any sense of adequacy to do it. "Let this cup pass from me" is much more characteristic of biblical prayer at its very heart than "Praise the Lord."

From the perspective of biblical religion, then, the heart of prayer is the issue of vocation, of living out "thy kingdom come, thy will be done, on earth as it is in heaven." Since we are still asked for prayers for vocations and the term is used for vocations to priesthood, it still needs to be reiterated that every Christian has a vocation, though not necessarily to be ordained or to live in a community that has an officially approved rule of life. It also needs to be noted that vocation is not the same thing as occupation or profession, though these are often described as being vocations. To put it at its simplest (though that is probably the most confusing way to put it), while we may be called upon to do many things, our vocation is simply to be ourselves. Vocation, in brief, is the priority or set of priorities that directs and shapes all the rest of my life.

Nobody's vocation is to be a doctor or a garbage man; it is the why and the how of my being a doctor or a garbage man that counts—though I may have a set of skills and opportunities that demands that (in my vocation) I indeed choose to become a good doctor rather than a good garbage man. To put it another way, the fundamental issues of power, sexuality, and death are the fundamental field of human vocation: how we deal with these is what our "calling" is about. To grapple with these issues in dialogue with the biblical tradition is to pray according to the canons of that tradition. It should go without saying, from what I have already suggested, that "dialogue with the biblical tradition" is not so simple a matter as using the scriptures as if they were a Sears and Roebuck catalogue of perspectives and behaviors to try on.

Authentic prayer is simply the grace of the Holy Spirit in us, as the Christian tradition from the gospels and St. Paul to Augustine and Aquinas has always insisted. Because of that confusion about what "personal" relationship with God means, and because our separation of Confirmation from Baptism makes us think that the Holy Spirit is some sort of special extra (around maybe to bail us out in time of trouble, or dropping in now and then to create a rush of enthusiasm), we have a very inadequate view of what the work of the Spirit looks like. A description from theologian Karl Rahner may help. Raising the question as to where we may discover the grace of the Holy Spirit, he gives the following suggestion:

> When a single sustaining hope enables us to face courageously both the enthusiastic highs and the depressing

lows of our earthly existence; when a responsibility freely accepted continues to be carried out, though it no longer bears any visible promise of success or usefulness; when a human being not only experiences but willingly accepts the last free choice of his death; when the moment of death is recognized as a fulfillment of the promise of life; when we no longer have any proof of the total value of our life's actions, and yet have the strength to view them as positive in God's eyes; when the fragmentary experiences of love, beauty and joy can quite simply be experienced as a continued promise of love, beauty and joy; when the bitter and disappointing and trying events of every day are endured serenely and patiently even to the last day, sustained by a strength whose source is forever elusive; when one dares to pray in silence and darkness and knows that he is heard, without thereafter being able to discuss or dispute his answer; when one deliberately embarks upon total retreat and can experience this as true victory; when falling can truly be called standing; when lack of hope can be seen as a mysterious kind of consolation (without any indulgence in cheap comfort); when one has reached the point of trusting all his certainty and all his doubts to the silent and encompassing mystery that he now loves above his personal achievements . . . This is where we truly find God and his liberating grace, where we experience what we Christians call the Holy Spirit, where the difficult but unavoidable experiences of life are welcomed with joy as challenges to our freedom and not as fearful specters against which we try to barricade ourselves in a hell of false freedom to which we are then damned."

This is an apt description of what it means to carry the cross of Jesus in obedience: it describes what "personal relationship" to God and his Christ in his Spirit looks like, and it thus describes what it means to be a person of prayer.

For all the silence of God, then, the possibility of prayer remains.

II

THE IMAGE OF GOD IN RITUAL PRAYER

In the last chapter, we named the problem of prayer in the modern world as an eclipse of our *images* of God rather than as an eclipse of God. In a changed and changing world, we are called upon to seek the face of God in mystery, to find God in the spaces between the cracked images of God. This poses a major challenge to Catholics, and indeed to Catholicism itself, because Catholicism is a sacramental religion. Its sacraments are themselves images of God. In fact, for Catholicism, they are its primary images of God. If you want to know what God "looks like" for a Catholic, discover what Catholics do in church, and what it means to them.

It may seem strange to speak of sacraments as "images" of God, so it will be worthwhile to explore here just how a sacrament is an "image to God," as well as to explore something of Catholicism's own understanding of its sacramental "system."[1] It will be worth beginning with a fairly obvious statement—that the compellingly attractive power of Catholicism does not lie in a superbly efficient organization (which is vastly overrated by those who do not know its organization well). And Catholicism is not especially attractive for its ability to compel assent to its teachings or directives. That ability is also vastly overrated, as

---

[1]The term "system" may not be an entirely happy one, with its overtones of bureaucracy or mechanical organization. But there are also biological and ecological systems, and this makes the term "systems" an appropriate metaphor.

anyone knows who talks to more than some narrow spectrum of Catholics. The much-vaunted "power" of the Catholic Church may sometimes be a political reality, even in the United States. But that power is continually hedged as much by dissent from within as by other forces from outside. The real compelling power of Catholicism resides in its sacraments. It is through its sacraments that Catholicism touches the hearts of ordinary believers. Sometimes, indeed, this is the exclusive contact Catholic people have with their church. Even in the United States, with a history of close and positive contacts between Catholic people and the organized church, and where there is often a deep sense of being and owning "the church," the touchstone of Catholicity remains participation in the sacraments, however minimally and however infrequently. Even in a country like the United States, where lay theological education is a significant fact of church life, and where participation in church organizations is much more evident than elsewhere, only a minority of Catholics bother with exploring the church's teachings much beyond the (somewhat forced) collection of childhood lore. And only a minority belong actively to parish or diocesan organizations and "work in the structure" in any way. The primary mode of belonging has always been and remains sacramental celebration, especially participation in the sacramental event we call the mass.

Often enough, this compelling power of the Catholic sacraments escapes helpful reflection. The old catechism definitions of sacraments may have been helpful for clarifying and codifying certain things about the sacraments, but they scarcely spoke very well to the believer's fundamental experience—that for all one's difficulties with the church, or its teachings, or oneself, the sacraments are experienced as an avenue into the mystery of God beyond the limits of the particular priest or place or way of celebrating them, and beyond the limits of one's capacities for entering that mystery without others who are also engaged in those moments of sacramental celebration.

From the believer's perspective, the sacrament is the "whole thing" (though often not named as such). The entire sacramental event—the people present, the ceremonies that are carried out, the lights, the vesture, the ornament, the very architecture of the

24

place, the song and words—all these together constitute a graced moment when there is a sense of access to God's presence and saving power. However important special moments within the sacramental event may be—the pouring of water, the exchange of vows, the consecration of bread and wine—the sacramental moment is not simply reducible to these moments, especially not from the point of view of the participant. Contemporary theology is more attentive to the participant's perspective, and is concerned less with pinpointing "what happens" in some single key moment or element of the ritual, than with seeing the entire ritual event as sacrament. And here again by "ritual" we do not mean simply ceremonies (though these are part of ritual), but the entire event as it unfolds. The very gathering of the people is "ritual," and the song selected by the musician is part of it, as are all elements of expression—from place, to ornament, to the moments of spontaneity—that inevitably form part of a sacramental event. Too close an identification between ritual and ceremony tends to cut the heart out of ritual. Rituals are the things we do. Ceremonies are the manners by which we carry them out. And sacraments are the rituals we experience as graced.

If the catechism yielded a set of definitions too narrow to name that experience of ritual prayer in common adequately, contemporary reflection often provides a set of "shoulds" that are equally inadequate to meet the believer's actual experience. Sacramental celebration, we are told, "should" be more of a celebration, "should" be more vigorously communal in nature, "should" be more inclusive of all sorts of conditions of people, "should" reflect adequately our own culture in its art, music, and general style. This is not too helpful to the office worker at a weekday mass among strangers in a downtown pseudo-Byzantine edifice, nor is it very helpful to the parishioner (whether bored teen or tired executive) who feels powerless before a parish that functions alternately as a spiritual bureaucracy and a village of cliques. While we can often be grateful for the many people and pastors who labor mightily to see that those "shoulds" are translated into reality, it is a simple fact of church life that they are not always observed. How does one continue to believe and hope and pray in the midst of something less than "good community"?

For it is the experience of many that the compelling power of the sacraments remains despite felt inadequacies of church life and celebration. The dogged parishioner who continues to "go" week in and week out while asking herself "Why am I here?" and those who choose not to "go" while left with a deep nostalgia for sacramental life, are both experiencing that same compelling power. There is something "there" that they seek or miss; in either case, it retains its hold on them.

This sense of the "something there" represents neither superstition nor nostalgia (for it grips people who are far from being prone to either), but is, rather, an intuition of the very heart of Catholicism. Catholicism is a sacramental religion. To describe it as a "sacramental religion" *does not* mean simply that it has a certain set of rites and ceremonies that it calls sacraments. It means, rather, that it understands *itself* as sacramental, as a point of meeting between God and ourselves. And in seeing itself as sacramental, it understands its very shape and structure as sacramental. Its rites and ceremonies flow out of that structure and form an organic whole with it. The traditional Catholic claim that the sacraments "work" *ex opere operato* (i.e., that sacramental action is an authentic point of meeting between God and ourselves where God's transforming power is accessible and available) is a claim grounded in the (often unvoiced) perception that the Catholic "system" is itself a place of meeting God and of being transformed by God's saving power. In a word, the sacraments come from the very heart of Catholic reality. Far from being "mere ritual," they are of the very essence of the Catholic "system." This does not mean, of course, that the rites and ceremonies of Catholicism were handed down from on high, cut out of whole heavenly cloth, though a more naive age tended to think so. Our rituals are human as the church is human, fully enmeshed in time, history, and culture, and fully mired in the darker human possibilities for missed opportunity, and for blindness and ignorance, to say nothing of occasional plain viciousness. From the giving away of brides like pieces of chattel, to the celebration of Easter as the "true" passover (with a clear implication that there must be a false one, and therefore prizing Christianity at the expense of Judaism), our rituals, like our church general-

26

ly, are marred and marked by human darkness as well as touched by divine splendor. This sense of sacramental action, as both revealing the glory of God in us and being marred by our own darkness, has been a perennial preoccupation of both theology and piety. The protestations of unworthiness that so filled the prayer books of the past, and still leave their mark on today's rite of mass, have had a long history in Catholic prayer. Likewise, the mystery of how unworthy ministers can administer holy sacraments has been a major preoccupation of classical theology.

The Catholic Church inherited from the Greek and Roman civilization within which it was born a cultural bias that often confused sacredness and unchangeability (i.e., what is oldest must be best). It also inherited from the same cultural matrix an assumption that basic institutions never change (i.e., the way we do things now must be the way we have always done them). Until recently, these cultural biases tended to block questioning as to whether the way we do things might be the best way to do them. They severely inhibited the ability to perceive the church, as an institution, as sinful. The natural result of this blockage of perception was an inability to conceive even the possibility that our rituals themselves might be in some ways inadequate and marred by human sinfulness. Modern historical consciousness and widespread modern rejection of Catholicism have begun to change that perception. Vatican II itself named the church, *as an institution,* as being sinful as well as holy. And the effort at liturgical reform is a practical admission of both institutionalized sinfulness and of institutional changeability. These admissions at the official level, however, remain to be integrated within our understanding of what we are doing in church. We are not a pack of individual sinners come to share in the perfect and timeless rites of the one, true church. Rather, we come together as a sinful yet graced people to share in actions that are limited and flawed as we are limited and flawed, yet graced as we are graced.

In the first place, then, a sacrament is an "image of God" for us, and a primary one for Catholics, because the sacramental act itself is experienced as an avenue of access to the mystery of God. If this happens to us as flawed people in the midst of a flawed

27

church, this is no block to the mystery. God meets us as we are, in this world. This is the very heart of biblical religion, a gospel three thousand years older than the advent of Jesus Christ.

Before attempting to bring this into sharper focus, it will be helpful to take a meditative pause. The sense of access to God in ritual prayer, as we have noted, spills far beyond what an older theology chose to single out as the graced moment. It also spills beyond what is officially labeled "liturgy," that is, the prayers, ceremonies, and directives spelled out in our liturgical books. And it is able to coexist with boredom, doubt, distraction, and the affront to one's sensibilities that any given event of worship may turn out to be. What follows, then, is a set of literary pieces that speak for that point of meeting between God and our lives that is the heart of religious ritual. These pieces are provided for the reader to savor, not dissect. In the Orthodox eucharistic liturgy, before the great eucharistic prayer begins, the choir bids the people to "now lay aside all worldly cares." This is not an invitation to approach the liturgy as an escape from life, but to lay aside all surface business so that life can be embraced more fully in the mystery of God. Ritual prayer is not a "hot" medium. It rarely yields instant results. It requires a different, more diffused and relaxed attention than the television commercial, the news announcement, or the inter-office memo. It is only in giving way to its totality, both its splendor and its pathetic limits, that we can find access to God in it. In the ecumenical creed (profession of faith) at mass, we are asked by the official text (though it is almost never observed) to bow when we affirm that God has entered into humanity and become one of us. Ritual prayer in community is a direct confrontation with that classic affirmation: it asks us to meet God in the human, in all its splendor and in all its limits. To do so takes, among other things, time and patience.

First, then, a reflection from Annie Dillard. Since Vatican II, one of the most exciting features of Catholic worship in this country has been its embrace of the informal and the ordinary within rituals that were formerly carried out as precision drills or performances of pomp. Often (not always), other "high" (sacramental) churches, e.g., Episcopalians and Orthodox, still carry out

28

their ceremonies with rather more drill and pomp, and with less room for the spontaneous and the ordinary. Many of my Episcopalian friends discover a "Baptist" quality in the way we American Catholics now worship. Likewise, some Catholics respond negatively to what is perceived as a "loss of a sense of mystery." Dillard's reflection on her experience of Congregationalist worship will, I expect, find resonances in our own experience of parish masses—as it suggests that the "sense of mystery" is not always best conveyed by pomp and precision.

There is one church here, so I go to it. On Sunday mornings I quit the house and wander down the hill to the white frame church in the firs. On a big Sunday there might be twenty of us there; often I am the only person under sixty, and feel as though I'm on an archaeological tour of Soviet Russia. The members are of mixed denominations; the minister is a Congregationalist, and wears a white shirt. The man knows God. Once, in the middle of the long pastoral prayer of intercession for the whole world—for the gift of wisdom to its leaders, for hope and mercy to the grieving and pained, succor to the oppressed, and God's grace to all—in the middle of this he stopped, and burst out, "Lord, we bring you these same petitions every week." After a shocked pause, he continued reading the prayer. Because of this, I like him very much. "Good morning!" he says after the first hymn and invocation, startling me witless every time, and we all shout back, "Good morning!"

The churchwomen all bring flowers for the altar; they haul in arrangements as big as hedges, of wayside herbs in season, and flowers from their gardens, huge bunches of foliage and blossoms as tall as I am, in vases the size of tubs, and the altar still looks empty, irredeemably linoleum, and beige. We had a wretched singer once, a guest from a Canadian congregation, a hulking blond girl with chopped hair and big shoulders, who wore tinted spectacles and a long lacy dress, and sang, grinning, to faltering accompaniment, an entirely secular song about mountains. Nothing could have been more apparent than that God loved this girl; nothing could more surely convince me of God's unending mercy than the continued existence on earth of the church.

The higher Christian churches—where, if anywhere, I belong—come at God with an unwanted air of professionalism, with authority and pomp, as though they knew

29

what they were doing, as though people in themselves were an appropriate set of creatures to have dealings with God. I often think of the set pieces of liturgy as certain words which people have successfully addressed to God without their getting killed. In the high churches they saunter through the liturgy like Mohawks along a strand of scaffolding who have long since forgotten their danger. If God were to blast such a service to bits, the congregation would be, I believe, genuinely shocked. But in the low churches you expect it any minute. This is the beginning of wisdom.

Often, of course, we are weighted down with the ordinariness of what happens in church—the blank faces, the inert bodies, the indifferent homilies, the inept readers, the unsingable songs, and the unfollowable musicians. And all the time, inside ourselves, we find a buzz of thoughts and cares that take us far from what we are about, or a numb emptiness that only heightens the sense of ordinariness and banality. The very presence of others can be a weight rather than a joy, and they need not be strangers to be such a weight. The problem of knowing those with whom one worships is, often enough, that their ticks and warts utterly overshadow any sense of the majesty or the mystery of the event at hand. Yet, often enough, it is in the midst of all this boredom and banality that the worshiper is suddenly surprised by joy and takes home splendor. Boris Pasternak admirably distils this sense of grace and grubbiness in his novel *Dr. Zhivago:*

> Lara was not religious. She did not believe in ritual. But sometimes, to be able to bear life, she needed the accompaniment of an inner music. She could not always compose such a music for herself. That music was God's word of life, and it was to weep over it that she went to church.
>
> Once, early in December, she went to pray with such a heavy heart that she felt as if at any moment the earth might open at her feet and the vaulted ceiling of the church cave in. It would serve her right, it would put an end to the whole thing. She only regretted that she had taken that chatterbox, Olia Demina, with her.
>
> "There's Prov Afanasievich," whispered Olia.
>
> "Sh-sh. Leave me alone. What Prov Afanasievich?"
>
> "Prov Afanasievich Sokolov. The one who's chanting. He's our cousin twice removed."

"Oh, the psalmist. Tiverzin's relative. Sh-sh. Stop talking. Don't disturb me, please."

They had come in at the beginning of the service. They were singing the psalm "Bless the Lord, O my soul; and all that is within me, bless His holy name."

The church was half empty, and every sound in it echoed hollowly. Only in front was there a crowd of worshippers standing close together. The building was new. The plain glass of the window added no color to the gray, snow-bound, busy street outside and the people who walked or drove through it. Near that window stood a church warden paying no attention to the service and loudly reproving a deaf, half-witted beggarwoman in a voice as flat and commonplace as the window and the street.

In the time it took Lara, clutching her pennies in her fist, to make her way to the door past the worshippers without disturbing them, buy two candles for herself and Olia, and turn back, Prov Afanasievich had rattled off nine of the beatitudes at a pace suggesting that they were well enough known without him.

Blessed are the poor in spirit . . . . Blessed are they that mourn . . . . Blessed are they which do hunger and thirst after righteousness . . . .

Lara started and stood still. This was about her. He was saying: Happy are the downtrodden. They have something to tell about themselves. They have everything before them. That was what He thought. That was Christ's judgment.

As Pasternak so aptly indicates in the preceding piece, one of the glories of ritual prayer is that it does not require that the worshiper be endowed with a special set of "religious" sensibilities. Part of its power to touch us lies in the fact that it helps all of us stand taller, whether or not we are especially pious.

The sense of "doing the right thing" by participation in a religious ritual often is enough to help us stand taller and find meaning in the midst of life's absurdities and pain. John Steinbeck dramatizes his insight into this dimension of religious ritual in the following earthy scene from *The Grapes of Wrath:*

"Think he's awright?" Ma asked.
Casy shook his head slowly. Ma looked quickly down at

31

the struggling old face with blood pounding through it. She drew outside and her voice came through. "He's awright, Granma. He's jus' takin' a little res'."

And Granma answered sulkily, "Well, I want ta see him. He's a tricky devil. He wouldn't never let ya know." And she came scurrying through the flaps. She stood over the mattresses and looked down. "What's the matter'th you?" she demanded of Grampa. And again his eyes reached toward her voice and his lips writhed. "He's sulkin'," said Granma. "I tol' you he was tricky. He was gonna sneak away this mornin' so he wouldn't have to come. An' then his hip got a-hurtin'," she said disgustedly. "He's jus' sulkin'. I seen him when he wouldn' talk to nobody before."

Casy said gently, "He ain't sulkin', Granma. He's sick."

"Oh!" She looked down at the old man again. "Sick bad, you think?"

"Purty bad, Granma."

For a moment she hesitated uncertainly. "Well," she said quickly, "Why ain't you prayin'? You're a preacher, ain't you?"

Casy's strong fingers blundered over to Grampa's wrist and clasped around it. "I tol' you, Granma. I ain't a preacher no more."

"Pray anyway," she ordered. "You know all the stuff by heart."

"I can't," said Casy. "I don't know what to pray for or who to pray to."

Granma's eyes wandered away and came to rest on Sairy. "He won't pray," she said, "D'I ever tell ya how Ruthie prayed when she was a little skinner? Says, 'Now I lay me down to sleep. I pray the Lord my soul to keep. An' when she got there the cupboard was bare, an' so the poor dog got none. Amen.' That's jus' what she done." The shadow of someone walking between the tent and the sun crossed the canvas.

Grampa seemed to be struggling; all his muscles twitched. And suddenly he jarred as though under a heavy blow. He lay still and his breath was stopped. Casy looked down at the old man's face and saw that it was turning a blackish purple. Sairy touched Casy's shoulder. She whispered, "His tongue, his tongue, his tongue."

Casy nodded. "Get in front a Granma." He pried the tight jaws apart and reached into the old man's throat for the tongue. And as he lifted it clear, a rattling breath came out, and a sobbing breath was indrawn. Casy found a stick on the

32

ground and held down the tongue with it, and the uneven breath rattled in and out.

Granma hopped about like a chicken. "Pray," she said. "Pray, you. Pray, I tell ya." Sairy tried to hold her back. "Pray, goddamn you!" Granma cried.

Casy looked up at her for a moment. The rasping breath came louder and more unevenly. "Our Father who art in Heaven, hallowed be Thy name——"

"Glory!" shouted Granma.

"Thy kingdom come, Thy will be done—on earth—as it is in Heaven."

"Amen."

A long gasping sigh came from the open mouth, and then a crying release of air.

"Give us this day—our daily bread—and forgive us—"
The breathing had stopped. Casy looked down into Grampa's eyes and they were clear and deep and penetrating, and there was a knowing serene look in them.

"Hallelujah!" said Granma. "Go on."

"Amen," said Casy.

Granma was still then. And outside the tent all the noise had stopped. A car whished by on the highway. Casy still knelt on the floor beside the mattress. The people outside were listening, standing quietly intent on the sounds of dying. Sairy took Granma by the arm and let her outside, and Granma moved with dignity and held her head high. She walked for the family and held her head straight for the family. Sairy took her to a mattress lying on the ground and sat her down on it. And Granma looked straight ahead, proudly, for she was on show now. The tent was still, and at last Casy spread the tent flaps with his hands and stepped out.

Pa asked softly, "What was it?"

"Stroke," said Casy. "A good quick stroke."

A well-known hymn invites us to "look beyond the bread you eat," an invitation that applies not only to the holy bread at the eucharistic table, but to all of ritual prayer. Part of the paradox of religious ritual is that, often enough, it is *itself* experienced or remembered as trivial, banal, boring, or all three. And so is the inevitable and integral companion of ritual—the reflection on it that is technically called catechism, the bits of love and reflection that attempt to name what the ritual means. It is a sense of the trivial that is one of the reasons that heartfully religious people can joke freely about their rituals, as they can about the catechism tidbits they learned. The child who hands you, chuckling, a Necco wafer, solemnly intoning, "The body of Christ," is not playing at blasphemy. She is simply telling you that she has grasped something of the heart of the thing—that in the midst of the experience of triviality and banality we find something great beyond words, to which laughter or tears, utter stillness or dance, silence or shouting are the only possible appropriate responses. Thomas Wolfe reflects this discovery of splendor in the midst of the experience of boredom, banality, and triviality in his novel *Look Homeward, Angel:*

> In the fresh Sunday morning air he marched off with brisk excitement to do duty at the altars, pausing near the church where the marshalled ranks of the boys' military school split cleanly into regimented Baptists, Methodists, Presbyterians.
>
> The children assembled in a big room adjacent to the church, honeycombed to right and left with small classrooms, which they entered after the preliminary service was finished. They were exhorted from the platform by the superintendent, a Scotch dentist with a black-gray beard, fringed by a small area of embalmed skin, whose cells, tissues, and chemical juices seemed to have been fixed in a state of ageless suspension, and who looked no older from one decade to another.
>
> He read the text, or the parable of the day's study, commented on it with Caesarean dryness and concision, and surrendered the service to his assistant, a shaven, spectacled, Wilsonian-looking man, also Scotch, who smiled with cold affection at them over his high shiny collar, and led them through the verses of a hymn, heaving up his arms and leering at them encouragingly, as they approached the chorus. A sturdy spinstress thumped heavily upon a piano which shook like a leaf.
>
> Eugene liked the high crystal voices of the little children, backed by the substantial marrow of the older boys and girls and based on the strong volume of the Junior and Senior Baraccus and Philatheas. They sang:
>
> "Throw out the lifeline, throw out the lifeline, Someone is sinking to-day-ee"—
>
> on the mornings when the collection went for missionary work. And they sang:

"Shall we gather at the river, The bew-tee-ful, the bew-tee-ful r-hiver."

He liked that one very much. And the noble surge of "Onward, Christian Soldiers."

Later, he went into one of the little rooms with his class. The sliding doors rumbled together all around; presently there was a quiet drone throughout the building.

He was now in a class composed entirely of boys. His teacher was a tall white-faced young man, bent and thin, who was known to all the other boys as secretary of the Y.M.C.A. He was tubercular; but the boys admired him because of his former skill as a baseball and basketball player. He spoke in a sad, sugary, whining voice; he was oppresively Christ-like; he spoke to them intimately about the lesson of the day, asking them what it might teach them in their daily lives, in acts of obedience and love to their parents and friends, in duty, courtesy, and Christian charity. And he told them that when they were in doubt about their conduct they should ask themselves what Jesus would say: he spoke of Jesus often in his melancholy, somewhat discontented voice—Eugene became vaguely miserable as he talked, thinking of something soft, furry, with a wet tongue.

He was nervous and constrained: the other boys knew one another intimately—they lived on, or in the neighborhood of, Montgomery Avenue, which was the most fashionable street in town. Sometimes, one of them said to him, grinning: "Do you want to buy *The Saturday Evening Post,* Mister?"

Eugene, during the week, never touched the lives of any of them, even in a remote way. His idea of their eminence was grossly exaggerated; the town had grown rapidly from a straggling village—it had few families as old as the Pentlands, and, like all resort towns, its caste system was liquidly variable, depending chiefly upon wealth, ambition, and boldness.

Harry Tarkinton and Max Isaacs were Baptists, as were most of the people, the Scotch excepted, in Gant's neighborhood. In the social scale the Baptists were the most populous and were considered the most common: their minister was a large plump man with a red face and a white vest, who reached great oratorical effects, roaring at them like a lion, cooing at them like a dove, introducing his wife into the sermon frequently for purpose of intimacy and laughing, in a programme which the Episcopalians, who held the highest social eminence, and the Presbyterians, less fashionable, but solidly decent, felt was hardly chaste. The

Methodists occupied the middle ground between vulgarity and decorum.

This starched and well brushed world of Sunday morning Presbyterianism, with its sober decency, its sense of restraint, its suggestion of quiet wealth, solid position, ordered ritual, seclusive establishment, moved him deeply with its tranquility. He felt concretely his isolation from it, he entered it from the jangled disorder of his own life once a week, looking at it, and departing from it, for years, with the sad heart of a stranger. And from the mellow gloom of the church, the rich distant organ, the quiet nasal voice of the Scotch minister, the interminable prayers, and the rich little pictures of Christian mythology which he had collected as a child under the instruction of the spinsters, he gathered something of the pain, the mystery, the sensuous beauty of religion, something deeper and greater than this austere decency.

The cheeriness of the Congregationalist minister, Lara's Russian Orthodox vespers, Steinbeck's salty Our Father, Wolfe's turn of the century Presbyterianism, all have their echoes in our own present experience of the Catholic sacraments, and especially of holy mass. The "image" of God is not a mental picture, but an experience of the mystery of God with us, which rises out of the wonderfully—and drearily—human encounter that ritual worship is. In these literary pieces, we can see, too, that ritual is not reducible to mere ceremony. The minister's booming injection of a "Good morning," Lara's chattering neighbor, Grandma's reminiscences of little Ruthie's prayers, Wolfe's Sunday school personalities, are part and parcel of the events that constitute moments of ritual prayer.

It is part of the special genius of Catholic (not only Roman, but also Orthodox and Anglican) ritual to prize and know how to create spaces of splendor and majesty—a genius that they share with Judaism. But when the majestic side of ritual pushes out all its other facets, the result can easily be an experience of empty pomp, of mannered oppressiveness, and of the alienation of faith from life. Far from sustaining a "sense of mystery," it can suggest that we can somehow tame and capture the mystery of God among us, putting God in God's place by performing the right rites. Alternatively, it can alienate the ordinary worshiper from a sense of the mystery of God in one's own life, effectively locating the presence of God among a select circle of religious professionals holding special sacred power. The revulsion of the Protestant reformers for the old Catholic rites and for the priests who performed them was precisely because in practice these had often degenerated into such empty spectacles.

With the coming of Vatican II and the official endorsement of change in the liturgy, Catholics began to give themselves permission to question a rather one-sided bias in favor of splendor and majesty in worship. They let themselves experience some of the same revulsion that Protestants had for ritual pomp. That critical spirit touched even the official level. In translating the liturgy into English, the translators deliberately avoided the stately and slightly archaic cadencing of the language that is still characteristic of the newest Episcopal Book of Common Prayer. For all the clumsiness this critique of splendor and majesty has introduced into our rituals (think of some of the wretched "folk" hymns we were subjected to, or of the studied cult of casualness some priests have adopted at the altar), it was a healthy opener to a richer sort of prayer that can more readily touch the hearts of ordinary people.

Still, there is much to be said for a touch of splendor and majesty in our rituals. God's gracious presence in our midst is a glorious one, and we must have moments of glory in our rituals if we are to experience that. Good ritual is not an exact mirror of "ordinary life," as we well might learn from oppressed people. The joy, exuberance, and expressiveness of Black Christian worship in this country rose out of an experience of "ordinary life" that lacked all of those qualities. The purpose of moments of splendor, majesty, and solemnity is not to mirror "ordinary life." Rather, their purpose is to point to the horizon and depth and ultimate meaning of ordinary life. In according grandeur to certain moments of ritual, we are saying that our very ordinary lives are touched with grandeur because they lie in God's embrace.

In consecrating bread and wine and oil and water, in sanctifying touch with sacred chrism, and smell with incense, the liturgy is not disinfecting ordinary things for special use. Rather, it is revealing the sacred depth at the heart of things. All our prayers of consecration, whether of the bread and wine at the altar, or

37

of the water of the font, or of persons (as at weddings and ordinations), begin with thanksgiving and end with doxology (praise), and speak for a world in which God is present at the heart of human life. Only magic and superstition attempt to summon an absent God to be present in a ritual event. Authentic ritual reveals a God already present in the world. Christ can only be present under the forms of bread and wine because we only find our full humanity in caring and sharing, and into that humanity God's image and likeness is impressed. And if our prayers of consecration begin in thanksgiving and end in doxology, they find their center in the invocation of the Holy Spirit. With images that recall the baptismal chrism as well as suggest praying hands spread over human head or gifts at table, the poet Gerard Manley Hopkins indicates the relationship between the ordinary and the holy that the liturgy calls forth:

God's Grandeur
The world is charged with the grandeur of God.
    It will flame out, like shining from shook foil;
    It gathers to a greatness, like the ooze of oil
Crushed. Why do men then, now not reck his rod?
Generations have trod, have trod, have trod;
    And all is seared with trade; bleared, smeared with toil;
    And wears man's smudge and shares man's smell: the soil
Is bare now, nor can foot feel, being shod.

And for all this, nature is never spent;
    There lives the dearest freshness deep down things;
And though the last lights off the black West went
    Oh, morning, at the brown brink eastward, springs—
Because the Holy Ghost over the bent
    World broods with warm breast and with ah!
        bright wings.

Of all the moments of solemn splendor in Catholic ritual, few are so majestic as the moment when the Easter candle is brought in procession through the church and the deacon stands to sing the great Easter proclamation, the exsultet. Yet that moment would not be complete without the light of the flickering candles playing on the faces of those present. The blessing of the Easter candle is a revelation of the light that shines in those people, even in all the darkness of their days.

Normally, the best ritual forms for evoking a sense of the majestic are the strangely familiar and the familiarly strange. They must wear the patina of age, yet be fully identifiable as "ours," familiar as beloved heirlooms are familiar. The nostalgia for Gregorian chant, while grossly exaggerating the role that chant actually had in Catholic worship before Vatican II, is not entirely misplaced. An occasional festive piece of Latin or a flourish of ancient ceremonial can, if used freely and expansively and without crowding out more ordinary elements of ritual, restore a proper sense of majesty and splendor to our worship.

Ritual prayer, then, has less to do with the performance of ceremonies than it does with the compenetration of the ordinary and the holy, the conjunction of the informal and the formal, the plain and the simple clothed in glory, the banal and the splendid joined together to celebrate God among us. *Sacram commercium*—a holy wedding was the term our Latin ancestors used to describe both God's taking on human flesh and the holy action of the common people of God we call the eucharist. Such it is, such are all the sacraments, such is all ritual prayer.

III

IMAGES OF GOD
IN THE TRADITIONAL ROMAN RITE

In the preceding chapter, we explored some of the ways in which ritual prayer presents us with an image of God among us, not in a mental picture, but in an experience of meeting God in the kind of compression of the human that a ritual event is. Rituals, however, do not float free from the communities in which they are imbedded. A ritual is always a ritual of somebody or some people. This is so true that people will tolerate considerable discomfort with a given pattern of ritual, as long as they think it is a necessary part of belonging to a particular group and consider it worth belonging to that group. And within a given community, the ritual clusters to itself the values most deeply held by the community. The experience of God in community is given its own particular shape according to what the community treasures most highly, and according to what it does and suffers while holding that treasure. The face of God takes on a specific shape according to the experience of the community as it prays together through history.

The paragraph above requires further reflection. In the first place, what has just been said is hopelessly abstract. It cries out for illustration, which we will provide shortly. Equally important, the sacramental event most Catholics call "the mass" is embedded in a particular historic pattern called "The Roman rite." We pray out of a pattern that had its origins in European civilization, and we pray as Americans who are the heirs of that culture, which left its marks on our pattern of ritual prayer, just as it has left its marks on the rest of American culture.

We also pray at a critical juncture in history. Marked as our ritual patterns are by the experience of the past, they are inevitably shaped by the past images of God, which fail in the face of contemporary experience. Yet our ritual patterns are not totally shaped by the past. With the movement for liturgical renewal that culminated in the reforms of Vatican II, we have seen a significant opening to the future. Enough remains of the old patterns to give us a link with the past, while the openings created by Vatican II give us room to find new images of God in our prayer. This remains, however, a task before us rather than a fact accomplished. As we said in the last chapter, we are called upon to seek the face of God in the spaces between the cracked images of God. And to say "we," means not a select and special few, but everyone who seeks to hope and pray and believe. In the long run, rituals are shaped as much by the countless, nameless millions who share in them as they are by their more obvious agents, the clergy and other ministers.

If we are going to reflect seriously on that particular pattern of ritual prayer we call the mass, then we need some understanding of the pattern in which it finds its home—the "Roman rite." As we noted in the last chapter, a ritual is more than the official ceremonies, and this is no less true of the "Roman rite" than it is of other rituals.

We need to begin, then, with some attention to the complex relationship between a community and its rituals. It can perhaps be best illustrated by an anatomy of a ritual form that once identified Catholics as Catholic, but no longer does so—the Rosary. Purists will tell you that this was a "private devotion." It is that *now*, because it is not a pattern of prayer shared by virtually all people who identify themselves as Catholics. To be sure, the Rosary was not a stupendously satisfactory form of public worship, but it was much more than a "private devotion."

In the first place, it was a form of prayer shared by all Catholics—devout and not so devout—priests, sisters, lay people, young and old. You could use it for every conceivable circumstance. It gave you a way of praying together when you were together, and it didn't require all sorts of bric-a-brac, planning or special personnel. You could say it three times a day or once a year, alone or with others. It was, quite simply, *the* common prayer of Catholics, their all-purpose liturgy when, for whatever reason, a sacramental service was not called for. Before Vatican II, it was so sacrosanct as a prayer form that even the most avid promoters of the liturgical movement always hastened to cover their tracks by saying a few words to the effect that, of course, they in no way wished to undermine the use of that most excellent prayer, the Rosary. All they did was insist that it was "really" a private devotion. People of a renewalist bent tried updating the Rosary with something called the scriptural rosary, a book of meditation based on the scriptures to use while you were telling the beads. This effort was not even popular enough for people to hate. The Rosary was so much part of Catholic life that somebody like myself, a new Catholic wanting to do the Catholic thing, went through the pains of the damned over not being able to relate to this form of prayer. Yet after Vatican II and the translation of the liturgy, use of the Rosary, except for a few hangers-on, collapsed overnight. People occasionally want it said at wakes,[1] and new Catholics, eager to latch on to all the "really Catholic things," sometimes ask about it. If, as seems entirely possible, there is an effort to revive it, it will be with all the flushed enthusiasm and doctrinaire brittleness that accompanies any movement to restore something that has seen its day.

Originally, the Rosary "took" because it clustered together

---

[1]The survival of the Rosary at wakes does not mean that people "really" want it at other times. It simply reflects one of the basic laws of rite—that even when rituals are abandoned for everyday use, they often survive at special times of either mourning or festival. The use of the Rosary at wakes is somewhat like the scattering of earth on the coffin at the burial, with the words, "Dust thou art, and unto dust thou shalt return," which in the Protestant churches survived even the Reformation. Originally it had been part of much more elaborate penitential rituals whose practice and meaning had long since been forgotten. These reliquary gestures have less some sort of literal meaning than simply the fact that they "mean" a sense of roots and belonging and history and purpose at times of deep grief or high festivity. And if they have lost their full and original meaning, it does not necessarily mean that they should be abandoned altogether.

42

a whole set of Catholic values into a prayer pattern that could be savored and positively appreciated by the simplest of folk as well as used by the more sophisticated. The legend of its discovery, and the origins of the Feast of the Holy Rosary, on October 7, are extremely important for an understanding of the "Catholic values" that were invested in that prayer pattern. The Rosary took the form known to us in the fifteenth century—a time of deep uncertainty about life, of a crisis of confidence in the organized church, and of the decadence of liturgical forms—on the very eve of the Reformation. The general social and political upheaval (England and France had gone through the Hundred Years War, and the English nobility spent most of the century slaughtering one another, unable to decide, until 1485, what family should rule.), the terror induced by the Black Death, and a crisis of all the forms of religion, made the Europe of the fifteenth century a world gone mad on death. This was the time of the dance of death, the proliferation of masses for the dead, and multiplication of chapels for singing those masses, which was to precipitate the Reformation with the fateful November of 1517. It was also a world gone mad in its preoccupation with human sinfulness, with its pervasive guilt internalized into a nagging insecurity about the afterlife, heightened to a fever pitch by all the other anxieties of the age.

In the midst of such a world, the Rosary came as a healing balm. At its most basic, the experience of saying the Rosary involves an experience of being "mothered," and not just because of the repeated invocation of the bible verse praising Mary for being the mother of the God-man. The rolling of beads between the thumb and forefinger itself has this soothing effect (think about Oriental worry beads). The very shape of the prayer is designed to give comfort and security. However well or poorly people were able to carry out the mental gymnastics of saying the Hail Mary prayer while meditating on the various "mysteries" (i.e., biblical and legendary incidents in the lives of Jesus and Mary), everyone was able to get the general drift of things. Instead of dwelling on grim forebodings about the afterlife, the prayer moved from meditation on the death of Jesus to meditation on his resurrection and ascension and finally to meditation on the glorification of Mary. The addition, normally in use by the sixteenth century, of the invocation, "Holy Mary, mother of God, pray for us sinners now and at the hour of our death," only rounded out what was implied in the meditations on resurrection while savoring Mary's maternal love—that here was a place of safety, and security, and hope. Moreover, at a time when the wealth of the church was the cause for deep revulsion, the most destitute could fashion beads of strings and seeds. At a time when ritual had grown complex beyond all imagining (it took close to forty-five minutes to get through the entrance rites in the English Sarum mass, the prevailing ritual in England), here was something simple and manageable, as well as satisfying and reassuring.

The prayer also served very well some of the preoccupations of organized religion. The legend of its being given to St. Dominic (founder of the Order that wore black and white and was in charge of the Inquisition) rooted the Rosary in a more secure and whole time: the "good old days" when the church was triumphant, Dominic's thirteenth century (still known to some Catholics of our century as "the greatest of centuries"). It also linked the Rosary with the cause of official orthodoxy. That link was redoubled when the story was spread that the battle of Lepanto in 1571 had been won because of the use of the Rosary to pray for its being won. Europe was under threat of "the Turk," i.e., of Moslem invasion, which was feared in the same way that Soviet invasion is feared in this country today. That battle definitively repelled the Moslem threat. It was all the more important a victory because the Catholics had suffered defeat after defeat in the years of the Reformation, with country after country falling to Protestantism. Lepanto was a Catholic victory in a century of Catholic defeat. If the Reformation rejected the Rosary as a piece of idolatrous superstition, this only served to enhance its value as a badge of defiance against what was seen as an alien (and dangerous) alternative to Catholicism.

In the succeeding centuries, a variety of other upheavals served to sustain the Rosary's utility. For instance, the French Revolution brought to an end the gorgeous offices of prayer in the French churches, yet people could go on saying the Rosary. An American

44

immigrant Catholicism, poor and on the move, could take the Rosary with it. An Irish Catholicism, deprived even of church buildings, could go on praying the Rosary.

Nothing hallows a prayer pattern like its use through loss and persecution. Up to the middle of the seventeenth century, a full century after the Reformation, Anglicans were extremely ambivalent about their Book of Common Prayer. They were racked between almost total rejection of fixed forms and a catholicizing element that would have preferred to restore much more of the old liturgy. But when the Prayer Book was taken away by the Puritans in 1649, and could only be used in secret or in exile, the Book of Common Prayer became "our incomparable liturgy." And when the Church of England came back with the restoration of the monarchy in 1661, the Prayer Book had to be reintroduced almost totally unchanged. Much of the same thing happened with our Rosary. It became, in the course of time, the hallowed survivor of many struggles.

Why, then, its sudden death with Vatican II? First of all, the death was probably not as sudden as it seemed to be. For a popular form to suddenly drop from use, it has to have already lost much of its meaning for people. Apparently, the Rosary was being used because it was viewed as "the Catholic thing," dutifully carried along because that seemed to be the thing that "good Catholics" should do. The liturgical change that swept over the church with Vatican II seems to have given people permission to quietly stop doing things that had already lost most of their inner meaning for people. This, surely, is what has happened with private confession. The sudden drop of confessions is attributable less to a sudden disaffection with the practice than to a recognition that it no longer serves as it may once have served.

But why should Vatican II have precipitated the final disuse of the Rosary? The description given of the conditions of the fifteenth century—social and political upheaval, uncertainty, morbid preoccupation with death (have you been to the movies lately?), general insecurity, oppressive guilt, decadence of ritual, mistrust of organized religion—sounds like a litany of our own ills. Add to this list church officialdom's preoccupation with orthodoxy and good order, and it seems paradoxical that the use

45

of the Rosary should have collapsed in our own time. One might think it would be flourishing everywhere.

There is, however, one item in its configuration that deeply runs against the grain of Catholic people today in this country. It lacks the democratic spirit; in fact, it fosters quite the opposite. Much of the message of Vatican II in American translation, said "democracy." "You are the people of God," priests kept telling us from the pulpit, "You are the church." At the same time, a liturgy that had for centuries kept people in a passive, penitential, and even fetal position, suddenly told us to stand up, make our voices heard, join in cooperation with our neighbors, and talk back to the priest. Out in the pew, you no longer saw "us sinners," but instead, "the holy people of God." There is a fundamental incongruity between this estimate of what it means to be a Catholic Christian and what it has traditionally meant to pray the Rosary. Mary has been portrayed in Catholicism essentially as the Obedient Woman, and that obedience has been consistently interpreted as a submissive obedience that says yes immediately, without question, without looking to right or left, and without the possibility of reconsidering. In a church obsessed with that style of obedience, the Mary of the Rosary stood as model of both believer and organized church. Her submission was seen as something to imitate, while the experience of being mothered allowed the pray-er to experience himself in relation to Mary (and by implication, to God and the church) as a submissive child.

This is not, of course, to suggest that everyone who keeps on saying the Rosary has an infantile piety or an "old church" notion of what it means to belong. People have their own private reasons for engaging in practices of piety, which are as varied as there are people. Rather, the Rosary has collapsed as a *public* phenomenon. The common values that it embraced are no longer viable in a configuration that presses the model of the Christian life into the model of a submissive obedience to figures of authority. A ritual pattern always clusters to itself those values that are seen as determining the shape of the community. In its exaltation of Mary as parent, and its placing the believer in the position of child, the Rosary was saying much about the way Catholics perceived the right ordering of the church—as a set of relationships between caring and commanding parents and obedient children.

We should note in passing that Jesus' choice of the title Father as his own preference among Jewish titles of God gives no room to press the metaphor of relationships between parents and children in relation to the ordering of the church. We owe that use of the metaphor more to the culture of Greek and Roman antiquity, and to the feudal age, than to our biblical heritage. The vigorous words of Jesus against the exercise of authority among the disciples as if it were military or political power indicated a definite bias *against* such use of the metaphor. Jesus' own saying, "Call no man father," besides disapproving of cult heroes and media personalities in the Christian church, also points to a view of the ordinary believer as a responsible adult.

Keeping that in mind, and observing how responsible adults behave and speak in relation to their parents, we may suspect that the proper naming of God as Father not only gives room to contend with our tradition, with our clergy, and with God, but actually demands it. The difference between grown children and strangers is that the stranger prefers silence and withdrawal to the tumult of real dialogue.

The emerging contemporary mode of believing (and hence of ordering the church) is one in which people are not prepared to see themselves as children, but wish to see themselves included as partners. For the same reasons that the Rosary has become unacceptable, so has a whole set of language and ways of doing things. No preacher attentive to a contemporary congregation would dare say "Holy Mother Church tells us...."

The Four Roman Rite Images:
Mary, the Bread and the Wine, the Passion of Christ, and the Pope

As we have seen in our anatomy of the Rosary devotion, a pattern of ritual carries with it the history of the people who use it, even as it gives them a sense of meaning and hope in the present. It survives in full vigor as long as it enshrines the values most deeply held by the community that uses it. As a form of

47

prayer, it names where God is to be found in the midst of life's trials and triumphs, and traces the contours of God's face as it is to be found in the experience of that people. For the most part it does those things without people self-consciously reflecting on them. Its greatest power is that it affects people at a level of knowing that is pre-reflective and intuitive. That is why most people are not able to give a very coherent account of why they do the things they do, and why those who try to give such an account are something of an oddity.

Conscious reflection, however, becomes necessary at significant points of transition. Traditional wisdom, enshrined in habits of thinking and acting, only works as long as the world in which the tradition was born remains in place. When that world dies, new questions arise that have never been faced before, and we have to ask ourselves why we have done the things we have done and thought the things we thought. We have to sort out what elements of the inherited wisdom we will carry with us and what elements we must discard as no longer fitting the new situation. This is the task we now face with our inherited ritual. It is put in our hands to do an immense work of reinterpretation, in ways of doing as well as in ways of thinking. In terms of the Roman rite, then, what was the "inherited wisdom," and what is the "work of reinterpretation" that we are now called to take on?

Let us begin with the "inherited wisdom." In our anatomy of the Rosary devotion, we saw a kind of miniature portrait of how rite works to give God a face in the midst of our history. This gives us some tools for reflecting on a larger, older, much more central, significant, and enduring ritual—the Roman rite of mass, the pattern of which we are the heirs.

The Roman rite of mass that endured until Vatican II was not, as some now choose to call it, the "Tridentine" mass (after the sixteenth century Council of Trent). It was the product of centuries of cultural and religious development. While its remote ancestry is in the Jewish tradition of festive meals, (reshaped by the experience of Jesus and his disciples, the apostolic church and the age of martyrdom) the contours of what we would recognize as the Roman rite were only beginning to emerge between the fourth and seventh centuries of the Christian era. Much of what older Catholics would identify as the "traditional" rite of mass emerged after that time, especially between the ninth and thirteenth centuries. While other features of the ritual still underwent change after that time, much of the ceremony remained the same from the thirteenth century to the present. The shaping of the ritual and ceremony from the ninth to the thirteenth centuries is of special importance, because it was during that time that the rite definitively clustered the values and images of God recognized thereafter as "traditional" by Roman Catholics.

It is not necessary to trace here the whole history of the Roman rite of mass to say what those values and images of God were. A reflective visit to an old and unremodeled Catholic church will serve the reader almost as well, and for the older reader, a journey in memory will do. Four images of God became the hallmarks of the Roman rite: you knew that you were at a Roman Catholic liturgy if they were there. Those four images were Mary, the bread and the wine (especially the bread), the passion of Christ, and the pope. It is interesting to note that while these things all have real honorable mention in the classic texts of the Roman rite, they do not stand out with any peculiar prominence in those texts. It was what piety accorded these things, and what architecture and ceremony did to respond to that piety, that made them the distinctive features of the rite. To this day, for instance, Catholics are disconcerted if there is not a fairly lifelike crucifix in prominent display in the church. Despite the insistence of many priests, all that is officially required is "a cross," and it need not be on the altar at all. The text of the medieval mass only mentioned Christ's passion three times. But from the ninth century onward, Catholics had been taught to think of the mass as a representation of the passion, and to meditate on each detail of the ceremony as if it called to mind some detail of the passion story. Altars were constructed to resemble tombs rather than tables. Whenever possible they were built over martyr's shrines, and where they were not, they still had to contain their relics. The actual physical icon of the crucifix (which only achieved real prominence *after* the thirteenth century) was only an outward manifestation of the image of the crucifixion that the mass was already experienced as being.

The identification of the mass as a representation of Christ's death was also given special prominence by the ever-greater multiplication of masses for the dead, which was one of the hallmarks of medieval piety. The weight of this tradition is still with us. Who would think of bringing a stipend to pray for the *living* at a mass? Just how deeply this identification between the mass and the passion goes can also be seen as an issue of theology in the controversies of the Reformation: one of the most deeply dividing issues was the relationship of Christ's historic death to the event of the eucharist. It never occurred to either side that the eucharist might be something other or more than simply a representation of Christ's passion.

The prominence of the bread and the wine scarcely needs commentary. From the ninth century onward, there was an ever more scrupulous and restrictive use of the sacred elements. Communion in the hand, the use of real bread, and the people's communion from the cup all died out, while ceremony and architecture ever more served to enhance that sense of the sacred presence. The offertory rite, originally a simple (and silent) readying of the table, became an elaborate preparation of the gifts for consecration, and every available space in the rite of mass was filled with the celebrant's protestations of unworthiness. By the thirteenth century, the rite of mass had developed into a ritual drama centered on the moment of consecration, carried out in a hushed stammer, and signaled by elevations and bell ringing. Piety had pressed these developments, and piety responded to them again: in the succeeding centuries, Benediction of the Blessed Sacrament became one of the most popular forms of devotion. By the seventeeth century, prominent reservation of the Sacrament on the main altar was mandatory. Most Catholics came to think of the church building as a shrine for housing the Blessed Sacrament, and doubtless they would find the assertion of the Catechism of the Council of Trent, that the church building is "the place where the word of God is proclaimed," peculiarly "Protestant."

Mary and the pope are, of course, different sorts of images than the passion and the bread and the wine. We have never made much investment in pictures of the pope in church, nor have we attempted any sort of theology of a "real presence" of Mary, at least not in the sane mainstream of Catholicism (both efforts have indeed seen historical, though mercifully limited, manifestation).

The Western church looked to Rome as its one apostolic foundation (and for the political validation of medieval monarchy, which was the church's patron). In a complex process of hybridization, the rituals of local churches appropriated Roman forms, not because they were told to by Rome, but because they wanted that link with the church of the Apostles. As the mission of Western Christianity pressed northward and eastward in Europe, monks under Rome's patronage took with them the hybrid rituals that had become identified as "Roman." That effort was reinforced later all over Europe when traveling friars, bent on the renewal of the church, again took with them the ceremonies, practices, and perspectives they had learned at Rome. And under the threat of the Reformation, Catholics again looked to Rome, not only for unity, but also for uniformity against the threat of dissolution. The ritual then was decidedly Roman, and not only in its Latin language. Its very shape, and ultimately, even the regulation of that shape, linked it with the See of Rome. The church may not have had a picture (or, often, even a flag) of the pope, but its ritual was papal through and through.

The relationship between Mary and the mass was, if anything, even more subtle (though no less real) than the relationship between the pope and the mass. Rome itself vigorously resisted the surge of Catholic interest in Mary that surfaced originally in the churches of the East in the fourth century. The feasts of Mary came late to the calendar, and only slowly found a home in Rome itself. In contrast to the effusive prayers of the East from the same period, the classic Roman Canon (c. 600) still only accords her a passing mention and hastens to add the names of the apostles. Ceremonially, Mary remained "on the edges" of the rite of mass right down to the reforms of Vatican II. Yet this was not the place she held in the hearts of ordinary believers. More often than not, medieval cathedrals were dedicated to the Virgin, and none would have been complete without its Lady chapel. A whole round of Marian feasts, daily offices, and pious

51

practices so surrounded the rite of mass that it became impossible (if not entirely logical) to think of the mass without Mary. Devotions carried out by ordinary people while they were at mass, such as the Rosary and others in conjunction with the ever more prominent physical icons of Mary (statues and pictures), inevitably gave the mass a Marian "feel." The typical English crucifix by the end of the middle ages, for instance, was a full crucifixion scene including Mary standing at the foot of the cross. Displayed as this normally was over the sanctuary gate, it could only speak for an indelible association between Mary and the mass.

The way a contemporary congregation can lustily greet its presider with "Hail, Holy Queen, Enthroned Above" and have no sense of incongruity, speaks for that association between Mary and the Mass which was at the heart of medieval piety and remained there ever after.

If these—the passion, the bread and wine, the pope, Mary— were the primary images, what was their value and how did they speak for the experience of God? In our anatomy of the Rosary, we have already explored some of the ways in which that devotion, and all devotion to Mary, made her an image of the experience of God. In a world weighed down by a sense of guilt, disorder, and insecurity, devotion to Mary spoke for a God of love and mercy. She gave God a maternal face. In a world that understood all hierarchy (not simply that of the church) as sacred and God-given, the affirmation of submissive obedience that was part and parcel of Marian devotion gave religious depth to a sense of duty and honor—which is why she was as often the patroness of knights and kings as she was of peasants. When the church and Catholics experienced themselves as oppressed and dispossessed, the stories of Mary at Nazareth and Bethlehem and at the foot of the cross spoke to that experience, too. And in a church where male and clerical domination was everywhere taken for granted, and where, during those long centuries, the laity were for all practical purposes excluded from full sacramental celebration, this woman, without power or influence, and without biblical record of her sacramental participation, stood as the glorious representative of all the unenfranchised people of God.

In many ways, the four great images of the Roman rite cluster

52

together: the values they enshrined and the meanings they bore overlapped and crisscrossed one another, so that to speak of the one is to speak of the other. This is only to be expected in a ritual pattern: the images of God that it evokes are parts of an organic whole, each endowing the other with meaning. It is especially difficult, then, to separate the devotion to Mary from the devotion to the passion that was so central to the old liturgy. In their fascination with the physical suffering of Christ, and in their love of embroidering details on the biblical accounts of his passion, our ancestors in faith were grappling with a sense of God's identification with human suffering, of God being on the side of the oppressed and the dispossessed, and indeed, of God's identification with all the pain of the world. They were grappling, too, with a deep sense of the life of faith as a struggle, as a life that costs and often costs dearly. And though it is often difficult to bend the contemporary mind to this perception, they saw Christ's suffering as the ultimate and awesome manifestation of God's care. Gripped as they were by an overwhelming (we would say morbid) sense of the majesty of God and of human insignificance, the thought of God taking on human form and enduring the suffering of the cross was a staggering intuition of love without limit. To fully appreciate the piety of our ancestors, we need to remember that for centuries the Catholic Church remained in the grip of a pessimism about the possibility of salvation inherited from Saint Augustine. Devotion to the passion came as an antidote to that extreme pessimism.

Devotion to the pope as a *person* is a modern phenomenon indeed: only modern communications media have made that sort of devotion possible. During the first wave of romanization of the liturgy, the pope was little more (personally) than a pathetic figurehead. The medieval papacy for a long time enjoyed immense political power and its power to protect the new religious orders that were the agents of liturgical romanization had much to do with the specifically Roman shape the medieval liturgy took on. But that phenomenon worked both ways. The new orders exported their feasts and devotions back to Rome, and the rite received as much from elsewhere as it took from Rome. The perennial value of the liturgy's distinctively Roman cast lay less in Rome's ability to impose its practices elsewhere than in Western Catholicism's constant Romeward look to the papacy as a center of apostolicity as well as unity. The link with Rome was both a link with the heritage of the past and a central bond of unity transcending local culture (and later, nationality). With its Latin language and distinctively Roman features, the liturgy of every little parish and isolated diocese spoke for links with a heritage greater and grander and older than local culture. As long as people thought of Europe as "the world," a distinctively Roman cast to the liturgy let it speak for a God who is God of all, and not simply of this little isolated people.

With the discovery of the New World and the beginnings of Catholic mission outside of Europe, it might well have seemed logical to question the thoroughgoing romanization of the liturgy. Indeed, the Jesuit missionaries to China did this vigorously, though without success. By that time, European Catholicism was suffering from the onslaught of the Reformation. The general result was a closing of official ranks against the Protestant threat. The Roman character of the liturgy was guarded as a hedge against heresy and dissolution. We began to prize uniformity as a badge of loyalty and orthodoxy. This may have been a colossal blunder, for it put our ritual, like the rest of our church, on the fringes of the life of the world—the inevitable result of a refusal to embrace the direction culture is going. This, however, is not to say that the thoroughly Roman liturgy that immigrant Catholicism brought with it to the United States did not serve it well. In a world where immigrants were treated as strangers and aliens, they could attend their churches with a sense of sharing a heritage that was ancient, grand, and above all, their own special brand of expression of faith. For God to be God for us, God must not only be the God of all, but also *our* God. In practicing a strange rite in an alien land, American Catholics were experiencing indeed that God was their God. And to stand with Rome was to stand with all the saints of ages past.

To reflect on the "meaning" of the special prizing of Christ's presence under the forms of bread and wine is in some ways a tautology: it meant, obviously, that Catholics believed Christ to be truly present in that way. And this does go to the center of the matter; for in the final analysis, it names God as truly accessible to us, and not only accessible, but radically vulnerable and involved in our world, present at the very heart of the material and the human. It is difficult to imagine an image of God that could be simpler, that could speak more directly for the divine presence to the created, the ordinary, and the everyday—an image as present indeed to basic needs as to highest aspirations. What is more basic than the need for food for survival, and what is more noble than the human possibilities of sharing and caring? To be fed is our most basic need in the Christian scale of values; to give oneself for those in need is the highest virtue. This was all the more heightened in the world that gave birth to our ritual. For European civilization (Catholicism in particular) remained haunted by a pre-Christian religious bias inherited through Greek and Roman philosophy—that there is something dangerous about the life of the body, and that "real spirituality" has to do with disdain for the world of matter and change, and distrust of the body. Anyone who knows the political or economic history of the Catholic Church would never guess that it harbored these dark suspicions about the world of matter, but nonetheless it was a fact of life whenever people became remotely serious about the living of the Christian life. It was there like a dark specter. Christ present under the lowly form of bread shone out as a revelation against that darkness. Eucharistic real presence spoke, and spoke dramatically, for God's embrace of humanity in all its fleshiness and materiality. As they bent the knee when the choir sang of God's taking on human flesh, Catholics knelt to adore the eucharistic presence, able to experience that this was the very heart of the matter.

The "loss of the sense of mystery," which many people report as their experience of the contemporary liturgy, doubtless reflects the power that the four great images of the Roman rite of mass had, not only to invite awe and wonder, but also to transform and sustain life in this world. For reasons that we will explore in the next chapter, liturgical reform has fractured our connection with those images, less by abandoning them than by disturbing their configuration. For reasons that we will also explore, that disturbance is both necessary and useful for the life of faith in the world in which we now live.

IV

FRACTURING THE IMAGES:
THE REFORM OF THE ROMAN RITE

Considered from the perspective of the official texts, liturgical reform has meant only a modest revision of the Roman rite mass. To be sure, there have been any number of significant additions—more readings from scripture over a three year cycle, and, instead of only one Canon, there are now eight new eucharistic prayers. A prayer of the faithful (general intercessions) has been added, and a few minor prayers dropped. But a medieval cleric thumbing the pages of today's *Roman Missal* would recognize its prayers as obvious relatives of the prayers he used, both in their arrangement, and, for the most part, in the very words he used in Latin. The ceremonial has been made simpler and more practical, especially for the priest. He makes fewer bows, signs of the cross, and crisscrossings of the altar. Altar servers have less to do than they used to. But the new ceremonial is a clear kin of the old rite.

Yet this modest change of ceremony has helped to precipitate a revolution in our ritual, a revolution so great that it has fractured a relationship that endured for centuries between ourselves and our images of God. How did it do this? And what was the point of it, anyway?

The real revolution was not this modest streamlining of ceremony, and certainly not the very cautious addition of texts and prayers that are in most ways harmonious with the ones we formerly used. The real revolution was that the agents of reform (who included, among others, Pope Paul VI) effectively abolished the distinction between sanctuary and nave, formerly characteristic of all Catholic worship and of the rite of mass in particular. In fact, there is no such thing as a sanctuary in the nomenclature of the new official books. To put it another way, the whole church has become the "sanctuary." The point was not lost on the architect who redesigned St. Paul's Chapel on the University of Wisconsin campus in Madison. He took the old (and beautiful) wooden communion rail and embedded it in the wall above the front entrance of the chapel.

Another way of saying this is that the reformers of Vatican II adopted the principle of "full, conscious, and active participation of mind and body" for the liturgy. This was the jargon canonized by the Constitution on the Sacred Liturgy in 1964 and by the General Instruction of the Roman Missal in 1970. But as we have more than suggested in the last chapter, ordinary Catholics through the centuries have always enjoyed that participation, however inert they may have *looked* to the casual and uninformed observer. In their own way, they made the mass their own, and it is an unappreciative travesty to describe them as having been "mere spectators." In their genius for creating and multiplying pious practices against prayers and ceremonies that through barriers of language and architecture kept them excluded, and in their genius for constantly reinterpreting those prayers and ceremonies through the lenses of their own piety, their participation was scarcely "empty, unconscious, inert, mindless, and disembodied"—which is what a plea for "full, conscious, and active participation of mind and body" implies. If that official jargon means anything, it means what other official directives clearly imply, and what Rome finally had the courage to say itself in its official introduction to the new rites of penance—that after a lapse of some thousand years, the laity are (at least in principle) re-enfranchised as co-celebrants of the sacraments, and especially of the eucharist. It is significant that the new liturgical books do not speak of the priest as "the celebrant." They refer to him as simply "the priest" or "the presider." The whole assembly of the church, clergy and laity together, is celebrant.

That principle of co-celebration was implemented in a practical

57

way almost immediately with the turning of the priest at the altar to face the people, with the introduction of prayers in the language of the people, and with the clear provision that people were to respond vocally to those prayers. There was some initial hesitancy about this (and well there might have been, for it was a revolutionary step). The Constitution on the Sacred Liturgy cautiously indicated that the parts that "pertain to the people" should be translated into their language. By 1967 it was self-evident that all the prayers of the mass pertain to the people. The eucharistic prayer (Canon), formerly the sacrosanct preserve of the priest, to be prayed silently by him, was allowed to be translated into the vernacular and prayed aloud. Moreover, provision was made for the inclusion of acclamations by the people. Acclamations are more than mere "responses" (though we have still not learned very well how to make them sound and be experienced as other than simple assents to the priest's prayer). They are in fact a mode of co-celebration, a way of vocalizing the assembly's full ownership of the prayer. The political analogy of voting for something "by acclamation" is far more apt than often-made comparisons between acclamation and cheering at games, or applause at the theater. By the time *The Roman Missal* of 1970 was approved by Pope Paul VI, its General Instruction (official introduction and interpretation) could say without qualification that the meaning of the (eucharistic) prayer is that the *whole assembly* offers the sacrifice.

The introduction of vernacular hymns at mass, formerly discouraged officially, was encouraged from 1964 onward, and so was the ministry of adults together with the priest. The lay reader was soon followed by the lay minster of communion. Often at local initiative, practices dead a thousand years came to life again—standing communion, communion in the hand, lay communion from the chalice (now permissible on Sunday in the United States, though still infrequently observed). The eucharistic celebration without the general communion of the people, still normal a generation ago, has become an extreme oddity. The "dialogue homily" became popular in small groups right after Vatican II, but the active role of the laity in the ministry of the word has so advanced that, by 1982, in its new official introduction to the lectionary (book of bible readings for mass), Rome unqualifiedly endorsed the possibility of lay preaching at mass.

All of these gestures represent a re-enfranchisement of the laity as co-celebrants of the eucharist. To be sure, many of these gains have met with resistance, local and official. But the general tendency toward that re-enfranchisement has ultimately found official endorsement. It is a sign that the re-enfranchisement has been taken seriously both at the grassroots and officially. Most of the changes now officially endorsed would not have happened if it had not been for grassroots initiative. In many ways, art and architecture have lagged behind the general direction to re-enfranchise the laity (more about this in Chapter VI, where we will examine the present mass ritual in detail). Most of our music remains ornamental rather that fully acclamatory, as most church renovation still fails to take the abolition of the distinction between sanctuary and nave seriously enough. We still "form" priests in isolation from the assembly of the faithful, encouraging them to think of the mass as theirs rather than ours. Yet for all these (understandable) lags and byways, the ritual has indeed opened up in such a way that it often is or can be experienced as an action of the whole people of God.

The present liturgy communicates certain important messages about the shape of the church as a people, and about the role of its ministries. Turning the priest to face the people, speaking to them in their own language, expecting a response from them— the ritual message is that the priest is a hearer as well as a speaker, not only a leader but also a partner in dialogue. The introduction of adult lay ministers into the ritual pattern also affects the ritual message about the nature of the church. As long as the only lay ministers were male children, dressed as miniature priests in cassock and surplice, and given the task of making the "people's responses," or helping the priest, the ministerial message was very clear: the role of the laity in relationship to the clergy was that of children to parents. The appearance of adult lay ministers with specific tasks of their own communicates quite another message: that the laity are partners with the clergy in a common task with both rights and responsibilities of their own.

The introduction of lay co-celebration effectively shatters the old ritual pattern, and hence the images that it generated. In the first place, it radically *localizes* the liturgy. The disappearance of Latin makes the liturgy an American or English or Papuan liturgy, not a Roman one. Add to this the "local color" of hymn selection, the special ways of doing things in this parish or that, and the liturgy is inevitably more "ours" in a very individual way. Local personality, individual and communal, finds a vastly wider range of expression in the liturgy than it formerly had. This contributes effectively to a fading of the Roman, and hence, papal image that the liturgy once carried. This is the reason why appeals to outside authority about details of practice are experienced as so incongruous and inappropriate now, where once it seemed perfectly natural to make those appeals. As long as the liturgy was Roman in tone and spirit, the official papal presence was as palpable as the mingled odor of varnish, beeswax candles and incense that used to be characteristic of Catholic churches. Now, that presence is considerably more remote or (because of the influence of the media) trivialized into a question of loyalty to a personality.

Second, the present ritual pattern makes it impossible to sustain the devotions at mass that contributed so much to making the other traditional images (Mary, real presence under the forms of bread and wine, the passion of Christ) alive in the experience of ordinary worshipers. Since the worshiper is now put in the position of being a hearer of the prayers and readings, and is expected to respond vocally to them, the texts of the liturgy take on a prominence they never had before. For anyone who attempts to concentrate on the prayers and texts actually being used, there is simply not the space to read a devotional book or tell the beads. This shift of attention especially affects Marian and passion devotions: the texts of the liturgy simply speak of too many other things. And while those same texts speak as much as they ever did for eucharistic real presence, the ceremonial unfolds less as an invitation to adoration than as an invitation to communion. From the preparation of the altar and gifts onward, the prayers speak of the sacred gifts as gifts to be received in communion: " . . . it will become for us the bread of life . . . to become for us our spiritual drink . . . ." With the priest praying the con-

60

secration facing the people, "Take this, all of you . . . " becomes a message that people hear, and hear enthusiastically. Where once it did not seem at all incongruous to "hear mass" without communion, full eucharistic communion becomes a felt necessity if one is present at mass now. Doubtless, one of the reasons that the issue of intercommunion with others has become such a popular one (and why it is so often practiced) is that the present ritual unfolds less as an event culminating in adoration and more as an invitation to the eucharistic table. Likewise, the exclusion of the divorced and remarried from the table becomes more of an obvious issue. As long as there was a less direct relationship between altar and pew, and where the celebration of many masses saw few communicants, those excluded could be present without such a terrible sense of exclusion at every celebration.

The ritual placing of the people as partners in dialogue with the priest, and the arrangement of ministries marking out lay people as co-responsible with the clergy for the life of the church, effectively shatter one of the deepest binding ties among the old images of God that were so powerful in the traditional liturgy. As we have indicated, the priest was ritually placed as adult parent to lay children in the old rite. This was much more than a ceremonial nicety. It presented an image of the relationships between believers that had everything to do with the way people were expected to relate to their priests, and priests to their hierarchical superiors. Office in the church was clothed with the aura of authoritative and sacred power, all the more reinforced ritually by the dramatic division of sanctuary and nave and by a ceremonial that was almost exclusively priestly and hieratic. The Christian life ideally lived was construed as a life of submissive obedience, and especially of submissive obedience to the clergy. Catechisms summed up the role of the laity in the church under the headings of the ten commandments of God and the six commandments of the church, speaking always of duties and never of responsibilities. Baptism was described in catechisms as making us "children of God and heirs to the kingdom of heaven," while ordination was described as taking on sacred power. The enormous role that confession played in the devout life served to reinforce this view of the laity as dependents of the clergy, and up to a generation ago, communion without confession beforehand was virtually unknown, if not entirely unthinkable. The power of the model of submissive obedience to authority as the ideal way of living the Catholic Christian life can still be seen in the shock that many Catholics still register over civil disobedience. The model of submissive obedience as *the* morality is so ingrained as to overshadow other moral issues, such as the horror of modern warfare.

This model of submissive obedience was deeply interwoven with the images of God that prevailed in the traditional liturgy. In our anatomy of the Rosary devotion, we have already seen how much Mary functioned as a model of submissive obedience in the traditional ritual. This was one of the distinctive features of virtually all Marian devotion. But in a variety of ways, this model of Christian life was interwoven into the other images as well. The distinctively Roman character of the old liturgy, especially after the Reformation, came to be appreciated almost exclusively (though not solely) as an image of submission to the pope, and sanctified by the blood of martyrs who died for the mass and for obedience to the pope. Devotion to the passion was also deeply linked to the issue of obedience: Jesus' endurance of the passion as an act of perfect obedience to the will of God (itself asserted vigorously in the biblical texts) was inevitably interpreted within the context of traditional relationships between clergy and laity.

In a more subtle, but all the more pervasive and powerful way, devotion to Christ's eucharistic presence was shaped in a way that reinforced the submissive relationship between clergy and laity. Since the ceremony of the mass unfolded as an action carried out by the priest, and since that ceremony was also shaped to find its peak moment in the consecration of the bread and the wine, the ritual was experienced as exalting the sacred power of the clergy. The theological locating of the "essence" of priesthood in the power to consecrate was only a reflection on the ritual pattern: that as the priest was perceived as having special power over the bread and the wine, so too he was perceived as having special power over the people.

In the traditional liturgy, then, the various images of God were bound together by an ideal model of living the Christian life in submissive obedience to authority. The images that touched the heart of human experience found focus in a valuing of a particular way of living the Christian life, a way of life that found vigorous expression both in ritual and in the everyday life of the church—in its patterns of living and teaching. The introduction of the principle of co-celebration into the new ritual effectively denies that old value of submission and exalts co-responsibility, partnership in dialogue, and a common mission for clergy and laity together. Tied as the traditional images of God were to the traditional model of submissive obedience, they are also effectively shattered by the abandonment of that model. The crises of faith, of authority, and of priestly vocations that have become acute in Roman Catholicism are the natural concomitants of that ritual disturbance. An eclipse of the image of God is experienced as an eclipse of God. The redefinition of priestly authority and power inherent in the new ritual inexorably calls for a redefinition of all authority, and for a redefinition of office in the church. It is difficult for people to respond to a "call to priesthood" when there is considerable (and inevitable) confusion as to what they might be called *to*. The cultural eclipse of the images of God, which we explored in the first chapter, is matched by an eclipse of the traditional images of God in the church's ritual.[1] In fact, that eclipse lies at the heart of its ritual, the mass itself. The need to seek God in mystery, amidst the shattered images of God, is as acute in church as elsewhere. Catholicism has embarked, after centuries of security and stability, on a quest for God in unknown territory. It is engaged in what can only be described as a grand experiment.

---

[1] One of the perplexing things about this situation is that the images of God are often confused with doctrine or belief. But it is one thing to believe in something, quite another for an image to have effective power in our ways of living, acting, and celebrating together. For instance, Catholicism believes in eucharistic real presence as much as it ever did, but it has significantly curtailed the ways of expressing that belief that gave eucharistic real presence effective power as an image of God.

This is why it has become so difficult to say what the mass "means." As long as the old images had effective power in Catholic life and imagination, it was easy to say what the mass "meant," for there was a direct and obvious connection between the prevailing images and Catholic life as it was actually lived. Now, there are any number of tensions, a tension especially between a large residue of old ways of thinking, perceiving, and acting, and new ways still in their infancy. That tension is as much a fact of ritual life as it is of the rest of church life. Reflection on the ritual must incorporate that tension (which is also a grand possibility for the future), rather than deny it or attempt to palliate it. The generation of people old enough to have experienced the ritual change in the church often complains that nobody adequately "explained the changes." But because the very nature of the changes was to place the church on a journey of discovery, it is for us to discover what the changes mean in the very living of that journey. In the fracture of the old images, there are possibilities for the development of new ones that will more adequately speak to our present situation in the world and in history. For the rest of this book, then, we will explore some of those possibilities. This inevitably puts us in the position of reflecting as much on what "could be" as on "what is." But this itself is to strike an effort at something that is perennial in biblical tradition. The God of biblical religion is the God of possibility, the God who beckons us into the future. To say that we "wait in eager hope for his coming" is to say that we are willing to look to a future where we will find God. To explore the "meaning of the mass today," then, is, inevitably, to explore its possibilities for meaning.

V

A NEW IMAGE: THE PEOPLE OF GOD

The reform of the mass rite was not simply a destruction of the old images of God. In fact, as we will see toward the end of this chapter, the present experience of their shattering has a potential within it for their creative recovery and reinterpretation. In the long run, they may appear to have been less shattered than significantly rearranged in the Catholic repertoire of images of God. In the ritual re-enfranchisement of the people as co-celebrants of the ritual, a new (to traditional Catholicism) image of God was being introduced—the assembly of the people itself. To abolish the distinction between sanctuary and nave and to make the people co-celebrants is to relocate the place of the holy in the midst of the assembly. Vatican II knew this very well, and from the Constitution on the Sacred Liturgy onward, official documents began speaking of the presence of Christ *in the assembly*. Those documents understand that presence to be as real and sacramental as the eucharistic real presence under the forms of bread and wine. When referring to that eucharistic presence, official technical language now uses the term "substantial" rather than "sacramental"—because all the modes of Christ's presence in the ritual (in the assembly, in the ministers,[1] in the word proclaimed, under the forms of bread and wine) are *all* real modes of sacramental presence.

All the inclusive gestures of the new rite speak for that reloca-
tion of the holy in the assembly. Vocal participation, lay ministers,
the use of the language of the people, communion in the hand
and from the cup, and all the rest, speak for an affirmation of
the whole people of God as a consecrated and holy people. The
old ritual communicated a profound sense of the presence of the
holy, but it was the holy defined as totally other and apart, a
definition of the holy that put a distance between the ordinary
believer and God. The devotions that were wedded to the rite
of mass, and thus formed an integral part of it, served—as did
the hieratic ceremonies and the Latin language—to sustain that
sense of the holy as other and apart. As much as devotion to
Mary might speak for the mercy and tenderness of God, it was
the mercy and tenderness of a God apart from ourselves. Virtually all Marian prayers spoke vigorously for Mary's sinlessness,
and by contrast, for the sinfulness of her supplicants. Passion
devotions sharply contrasted human waywardness and the rejection of God with Christ's meekness, obedience, and perfect con-
formity to the will of his Father. The fervent devotion to the
Blessed Sacrament only rarely impelled people to communion.
Centuries of Catholics who devoutly returned to the church on
Sunday evening for Benediction considered weekly communion
a mark of rare and unusual piety. For all practical purposes,
prayers of praise and thanksgiving were absent from the repertoire of piety. The prevailing tone of all devotions was the bewail-
ing of human sinfulness.

To this day, in the rite of mass, the better part of the people's
responses speak more for human sinfulness than for the sanctity of the people as God's beloved, as also do the official prayers
the priest says silently. The ordinary practice of the confessional
served to keep alive people's definition of themselves as sinners.
Because of its concentration on moral and ritual minutiae as

---

[1]Note, too, that according to the official liturgical books, it is not simply the
priest who "represents Christ," but all the ministers and the assembly of the
people. This authoritiative teaching is vastly underplayed in the Declaration
of the Congregation of the Doctrine of the Faith against women's ordination.
And the official liturgical books (like the Constitution on the Liturgy) have
greater official authority than the declaration of a Roman Congregation.

"mortal sins," the average believer was effectively schooled to think of herself as constantly hopping in and out of the "state of grace," and more *out* than *in*. This scarcely contributed to people experiencing themselves as a consecrated people. Devotion and ceremony both conspired to locate the holy as apart from the people. Much of the "sense of mystery" associated with the old rite of mass lay in its power to evoke a sense of the holy as *holy other*. The limit of this location of the holy was its inevitable separating of life from liturgy, of religion from everyday life, and of the church from the world. And its tragic shadow has been a common perception of organized religion as being mainly in the business of generating guilt.

The old catechisms described baptism as making us "children of God and heirs of the kingdom of heaven." The language is biblical, but in the context of traditional church life, it speaks worlds for the disenfranchisement of the ordinary believer as a consecrated person (which also enters strongly into the biblical understanding of baptism). Nothing in that definition speaks for adult mission in this world. Ritually, the holy was defined as the holy other, and as a consequence, the holiness of the laity was seen as a deferred holiness, something more for the next world than for this. The devotion to the saints and the cult of the dead, characteristic of traditional Catholic life, spoke for that deferred holiness. The preciousness of the saints who had gone before took precedence over the preciousness of the saints in the nave. The preoccupation with law characteristic of Catholic moral teaching up to a generation ago was part and parcel of that deferred and distant holiness. The living of the Christian life in this world was seen all too exclusively as a time of trial for which the ordinary believer would be rewarded, punished, or pardoned at the end.[2]

[2]It is worth noting that the whole life of prayer was itself seen in the framework of deferred rewards. The perception of Sunday mass as an "obligation" rather than a celebration was only part of it. Virtually every prayer (however private) considered worth saying came to have an "indulgence" attached to it. The word "indulgence" literally means "pardon." The need to have a reward in the next life attached to the prayer, if that prayer is to have value, speaks strongly for the valuing of the ordinary Christian life as something deferred to the next world. By way of contrast, Israel prayed for century upon century with no hope at all for an afterlife.

This catalogue of the limits of traditional Catholicism would only be a parody of its real life if we did not keep in mind its more positive side, which we explored in the chapter on traditional images of God in the Roman rite. There were a variety of ways in which traditional Catholicism, and Catholics, constantly transcended those limits. The journal of Pope John XXIII, *Journal of Soul,* when compared with his life as the world knew it, is a fascinating study in the transcendence of those limits. But limits they were, and they were the dark shadows of the old images. God, however, is always greater than the images of God, and access to God is always wider than the limits of the images we use.

To ponder the limits of the old images is not simply an indulgence in sour grapes. Because the church is human and sinful, it will always generate images that are less than perfect, less than adequate. Whatever images of God we generate will have their dark sides. There should be some real comfort in knowing that the much-vaunted "perfection" of traditional Catholicism had its dark side. Our ancestors in faith did not have some sort of ageless wisdom that we lack. Rather, we, like they, are called upon to find God in the world as we know and experience it. And we, like they, will be called upon to grapple with our own limits and transcend them.

A Case Study in New Piety

As we have strongly suggested in the preceding chapters, "devotion," or what takes place in the minds and hearts of the worshipers, is as important to the "meaning" of a ritual as the ceremonies performed. The images of God that are imbedded in a ritual, and that give the ritual substance and power, do not simply reside in the doing of the rite. It is superstition and magic to accord a rite power through the simple doing of it without reference to what it means to the worshipers and without reference to what it means for the presence of the mystery of God in their lives. A ritual has substance and power only when it has meaning for those who participate in it. The ritual re-enfranchisement of the people as co-celebrants can only function as a significant image of God present among us to the extent that we learn to treasure the holy assembly as we treasure the holy priesthood or the holy altar, or any of the other ritual elements that we have traditionally seen as manifestations of the holy.

Let us ponder for a moment the ceremonial timidity with which we often affirm the re-enfranchisement of the people as co-celebrants. Although we have turned the priest around to face the people, we have scarcely taxed our imaginations on how we might more effectively turn the people toward one another. The worshiper in the conventional pew is visually isolated from everyone except the ministers—a tragic discord for a religion that so highly prizes the visual and the visible as a manifestation of the holy.

While new churches have been sparing of statues and have removed the Blessed Sacrament as a center of visual focus during the event of mass, there is normally a space clearly defined as the "sanctuary" apart from the assembly of the people. The new liturgical books indeed accord special places for the seating of the clergy (the presider's chair and the "presbyterium"), for the reading of the Word of God (the Latin term is *ambo*, which should be an honored *place* rather than a simple bookstand), and of course, for the altar. But what they have in mind is a visual setting in which these necessary elements of the ritual *rise from the midst of the assembly*, rather than appearing as things that are to be placed within some special part of the church building. Worst of all, the baptismal font has come out of its backroom closet only to become one more piece of occasional sanctuary furniture. And we have not even given a thought to what it might mean to absolve people from sin in the midst of the assembly.[3] The general result is that the conventional parish church still defines the worshiper more as an individual, participating spectator than as a co-celebrant in union with other co-celebrants.

---

[3]The "confessional room" humanizes the encounter between the penitent and the one hearing confessions. But if we are ever going to celebrate forgiveness, it would be much more appropriate for people to come forward to be absolved (though not have their confessions heard) in the view of the praying assembly.

Although there have been steady gains in the development of lay ministries in sacramental celebration, the ministry of the laity to one another remains feebly signaled in ritual. Our inhibiting architecture is not the least of the reasons for this. The architectural isolation of the worshipers from one another positively fosters individualism rather than a sense of community. The sheer number and quantity of prayers that the priest is required to say aloud inhibits the possibilities of both common silence and common song, which are at the heart of true communal prayer.

Along with common action, song is the normal vehicle of true public and communal prayer. Recitation is an extremely feeble medium for a sense of co-celebration in a large group, except for a few formulae like the Lord's Prayer. A real prizing of the assembly requires a prizing of the ministry of music—which for the most part we have yet to learn how to do.

It is not only a lack of investment in time, money, and effort in the ministry of music that shadows our worship. Most of the "people's parts" (responses and acclamations, the profession of faith or creed and the *Gloria*) cry out for creative reinterpretation so that they can be truly popular. That reinterpretation would mean adjusting the text, composing appropriate musical settings and developing the kind of musical leadership that would make them work. Yet we remain nailed to wooden recitation, or at best, indifferent musical settings.

There is also a noticeable lack of lay pride in what we do in church. People will tolerate leaflet missals on cheap newsprint while gorgeous books are used at the altar, just as they will think nothing of attending the most solemn events of the liturgical year in the most casual of clothing. While much could be said about the legalistic silliness with which we approached fasting in the past, the lack of any real fasting before celebration inevitably trivializes sacramental events, so that comfort and convenience become the overriding concerns. And although much can be said in favor of the more relaxed manner in which we now behave in church, an absence of effective people's gestures (like the raising of hands in prayer, at least for key moments like the prayer of the faithful or general intercessions, the beginning and end of the eucharistic prayer, and the Lord's Prayer) suggests something

70

other than a sense of full co-celebration in the event of worship.

To catalogue these deficiencies, however, is not to bewail opportunity lost or to lament closed possibilities. It is only to suggest that the full enfranchisement of the people as co-celebrants awaits further development. To the extent that the ritual, as presently experienced, does not speak fully for lay enfranchisement, it weakens the experience of the people as the image of God. But that is not to say that there is not a piety developing that appreciates the assembly of the people as the image of God. Quite the contrary. A variety of movements are alive in the church that contribute vigorously to the development of a piety that values the assembly of the people as the image of God. The "new liturgy" had no sooner begun to be introduced, and the old devotions begun to wane, than a variety of popular movements sprang up that vigorously affirmed the emerging new image of God. And like the movements of popular piety that continually swept the Catholic Church during the past thousand years, these movements will ultimately have their impact on the shape of the ritual, both in its form and in its meaning.

As we have done an anatomy of Marian devotion, it will also be useful to do a reflective "case study" of one of those new movements—charismatic renewal. Any number of other movements could be chosen just as well, but the charismatic renewal serves as a helpful example, as much by its deficiencies as by its positive possibilities. Birth is a messy, painful, and often perplexing process, and the birth of a new Catholicism is no exception.

In terms of the old images of God and the model of Christian living that traditional Catholicism offered, an appreciation of the assembly of the people itself as the image of God requires a transformation of religious consciousness. As we have already noted, the general effect of the traditional Catholic system tended toward a vision of ordinary lay life as in many ways outside the sphere of the holy. For lay people, that system tended toward a conventional religiosity in which religion had certain basic functions touching important parts of life, but certainly not all of it. From the point of view of that conventional religiosity, religion had mainly to do with providing a dimension of the sacred to such key moments as birth, marriage, and death, besides functioning as a mainstay of duty and a comfort in time of crisis.[4] In a word, conventional religiosity defines religion as a part-time occupation, albeit an important part-time occupation. To be "religious" is either to be a specially set apart person (priest or person in special vows) or to have a special preoccupation with religion.

But for the charismatic, religion is a delight, not a duty, and it embraces the whole of life. The charismatic's religious horizon includes a vivid sense of wholeness, freedom, meaning, joy. The characteristic "Praise the Lord!" is a witness to that sense, an emblem of a wholly different sort of religiosity than that represented by the murmured responses and petitions of conventional piety. The interminable testimonies of charismatic literature and prayer meetings, with their stories of healing and deliverance, point to that new-found sense of wholeness and freedom. While the God of conventional religiosity works through carefully established channels and is met at special times and places, the God of charismatic renewal is to be met everywhere and anywhere. Sometimes, this is trivialized ("The Lord healed my head cold" or "I feel called to pour the coffee this evening"). But it also has a potential for new life and vitality. The conventional barriers surrounding the sacred are broken down. The whole of life is potentially the domain of the holy. The individual is seen as a sacred and consecrated person ("Spirit filled," "baptized in the Spirit") in a community of sacred persons. Through shared prayer, shared reflection, and shared interpretation of

[4]Readers may see nothing especially "Catholic" in this estimate of religion, though that is still the prevailing estimate of it in our very Protestant American culture. But this was Protestantism's heritage from medieval Catholicism. It is a testimony to the power of Catholicism's system to survive its political, doctrinal and ritual dissolution with the Reformation. The Reformers had something very different in mind than what conventional Protestantism became. The Reformers had *more* in mind what has been happening to Catholicism since Vatican II, which in part represents an embrace of their ideals and aspirations, and even some of their most characteristic doctrines (the priesthood of all believers, the church is always in need of reform, and a number of other central points).

scripture, all carry on a ministry with and for one another. Most important, the effective transmission of Spirit baptism requires no special class of persons. All may spread the message, all may pray for the gift of the Spirit, and all may lay on hands. The charismatic assembly in a real sense constitutes a para-church, and it is able to constitute it without benefit of clergy. The interplay between the use of scripture and the mutual ministry of the charismatic community reinforces and develops that sense of a para-church. Individuals understand themselves and their lives as identified with the biblical story. The biblical story is read, not as past event, but as a mirror of present experience. In a real way, "apostolic succession" is immediate: the community experiences itself as if it were contemporary with the churches of the New Testament.

Within this setting, the role of priestly mediation and authority is inevitably transformed. Nothing so well supports priestly power and nothing better highlights the role of priestly mediation than the patterns of conventional religion. A piety that is content to have its God move through carefully ordered channels is equally content to have its clergy marked out as sacred persons apart from the rest of the (not-so-sacred) community. Within charismatic communities, even when there are priests, both authority and responsibility are actively shared. The prizing of the intuitive (what charismatics call "prophecy") and of mutual ministry mean that authority is both localized and diffused: decisions rise out of community consensus, by complex and largely unarticulated processes. The possibility arises for an exercise of authority grounded in communal wisdom rather than in the power to command.

Often enough within the movement, this tendency toward a new kind of exercise of authority is co-opted by a lay para-clergy that rules more rigidly than priests ever thought of doing. But the vigor of this reactionary backlash is itself a testimony to the attractive power of an authority grounded in a common wisdom. The pentecostal experience seems to give people just enough taste of that kind of authority for them to want to see more of it.

Finally, phenomena such as speaking in tongues or the emotional ebullience characteristic of most charismatic assemblies have their own radicalizing potential. Such things are a bizarre affront to conventional religiosity. In fact, any sort of excitement about religion fractures a cultural taboo. The result is that charismatics learn to experience themselves as countercultural, an experience reinforced by biblical language about the cleavage between the Christian and "the world."[5] The conjuction of people's experience of themselves as a holy people and their finding that experience countercultural has explosive potential indeed. It readily leads to the heartfelt conviction that the authentically religious can and ought to be critical of the cultural, social, political, and economic status quo. However narrowly this opposition between church and world may be interpreted within the confines of certain charismatic communities, it still cracks the frequent supposition that church and dominant culture go hand in glove.

Charismatic renewal can be incredibly narrow, and often enough, downright silly. Yet it provides a taste of religious community that is authentically lay-based. It redefines the church. From a view of the church as a sacred agency providing certain services to meet certain needs, people come to an ideal of church as a familial zone of freedom, wholeness, and meaning. The charismatic assembly is a training ground for mutual and informal ministry. This makes it a zone for the potential redefinition of the sacred and of authority. It provides at least an initial experience of the life of faith as countercultural, thus opening people to the real possibilities of a sense of mission.

More than that, charismatic renewal provides a rich vocabulary that both sustains and legitimates a redefinition of the church. For centuries, religious language has been in the hands of hierarchical authority in Roman Catholicism. From the sixteenth century down to Vatican II, even the simplest private prayer had to have official ecclesiastical approval. In charismatic renewal, a whole language of devotion and practice has developed out-

---

[5]"The world" that the bible rejects is not God's good creation (which includes human art, skill, striving, and intelligence), but the sinful world, the world as it is less than whole, the world of illusion and misdirected power, the world of oppression, poverty, disease, and death.

side the control of that authority. However clumsily and crudely, it finds its ground in a source more sacred than any episcopal letter or papal document: the text of scripture itself. It allows ordinary people to name themselves as the holy people of God, and to do it in their own language.

The transforming potential of the movement has largely been co-opted within the movement itself. Its potential for the freedom of the people of God often sours into narrow fundamentalism, myopic pietism, or a rigid kind of control over the members of communities. But to look only at this is to discount the constant hemorrhage of membership from the ranks of charismatic renewal into other zones of renewal in the church. For such people, the movement is the seedbed for a lay leadership in a kind of church that is beginning to come to birth.

Equally important, in this case history, we can perceive the common converging lines between all sorts of lay movements in the church today. Religion is redefined as touching all of life, ministry is experienced as the common task of all, and a common and popular language emerges that prizes the people of God as a primary image of God's presence in the world. As the experience of these groups matures and has its impact on the larger church, that image becomes more and more powerful in the hearts of ordinary believers.

The Consecration of the Holy People of God for Mission in the World

It is often said that the real problem with contemporary liturgical celebration is one of "community"—that if the inclusive gestures of the ritual that speak for the laity as co-celebrants of the eucharist are to carry meaning and power, then we need a sense of "community" with one another. This is true enough, but such a hazy naming of the issue is not very helpful. It is especially unhelpful in an American context where an easygoing folksiness can be too readily and facilely identified as a "sense of community" while masking a cult of insularity, cliquishness, and even bigotry. As we have suggested all through this book, Catholicism

75

functions as a particular *kind* of community. What constitutes the shape of the community is all important. The church is a community of shared values and ideas; these are its fiber and backbone.

If that community which is the church is to value the people of God themselves as an image of God in the world, then its people need to know who they are, and to prize and cherish who they are. As we have already indicated, both the present ritual and contemporary lay movements contribute to that prizing and cherishing of ourselves as a consecrated people. But for a sacramental religion like Catholicism, this must take significant ritual shape, not only at mass but in other key rituals as well. The images of God and the model of the Christian life that the mass ritual clusters to itself are not sustained only by the mass ritual. They are also sustained by the *rituals of entrance*, which give access to full participation in the mass ritual. Here, we do not mean the "entrance rites" of the mass itself (though they are not unrelated to this question, as we will see in our commentary on the rite of mass), but those rituals that enfranchise us as full eucharistic participants—baptism (and with it, its consecratory completion, confirmation) and reconciliation.

In traditional Catholicism, baptism faded to a minor though necessary quasi-private ritual, as confirmation became a minor afterthought. The sacrament of penance grew more and more in importance in the life of the church. Where an earlier tradition reserved sacramental reconciliation for very special and extreme cases, and where ordinary practice had been mainly informal (including considering confession to another lay person perfectly normal and quite sufficient), traditional Catholicism made confession to a priest mandatory, and made the regular practice of it normative for church life. This fit perfectly the definition of the ordinary believer mainly as sinner and subject of the clergy's care. It became the regular and perceptible ritual entrance into full sacramental life, and worked very well within the traditional model of church life. And certainly, the current decline of confessions speaks for the breakdown of that traditional model. Within a pattern of piety that defined the laity simply as "us sinners," the prominence of the confessional in church life made eminent sense.

But if we are to perceive the laity as a consecrated people, as co-responsible co-celebrants, questions need to be asked about the adequacy of older patterns. Liturgical reform has enriched the ceremonies for the baptism of infants, just as the current practice of the sacrament of reconciliation, whether in the "room" or in "communal penance services," has been somewhat updated. Considerable effort has been pumped into seeing confirmation as a "sacrament of adult maturity"—a somewhat incredible effort, since it comes at or before the onset of adolescence, and often is simply a celebration of the end of childhood catechetics. It is also a somewhat dubious theological effort. The separation of confirmation from baptism is a historical accident. What our remote ancestors in the faith understood as "baptism" were different aspects of what we would call baptism-and-confirmation-together.

The problem with our rituals of entrance is that they normally occur in childhood, and they sound an uncertain trumpet regarding the status of the adult laity as fully enfranchised co-responsible members of the church. What is clearly called for is a public ritualization of the initiation of adults. This is not to say that all Catholics need to be baptized and confirmed in adulthood, but only to say that we need the public witness of those struggling to become full adult Christians, not only for their own sake, but for the sake of everyone. We need, in brief, to know what it looks like to become a fully enfranchised co-responsible member of a church that experiences itself as sharing a common mission. We need that witness both from those who are coming to faith for the first time *and* from those who are returning to reclaim their birthright. If we are going to appreciate ourselves as a holy people, we need to see what that looks like in the flesh.

And this is not to suggest only that converts to the faith should be publicly baptized or that returnees should be publicly reconciled. Adult conversion is a process that takes place by stages, and we need the ritual witness to those stages. Earlier, we noted the need to turn toward one another as well as toward the priest if we are to find God's holiness present among us. Nothing so calls an assembly of believers to a sense of the life within it as does the witness of those who find themselves impelled to share that life. And this is already the present experience of those parishes that are struggling to adopt and adapt the new rites of initiation and reconciliation to the life of the church today.

Toward a Recovery of Traditional Images of God

As we observed in the first chapter, a major factor in the eclipse of the image of God in the world is the shifting of the human experience of power: we are powerful in ways in which the race was never powerful before, and at the same time we are made helpless by the very work of our hands, which so often seems to elude our grasp and run amok. We might also add that traditional Catholicism's own power lay in its creative answer to the perennial dilemma of human power and powerlessness as it took shape in a world very different from our own. Traditional Catholicism could oppose the might of greedy princes as it could assure the simplest peasant of a place in the grand scheme of things.

The struggle to recover the image of God in the holy people of God is a struggle to make the church a zone of freedom, meaning, and wholeness. It is an effort to give people a place to stand where they can have a sense of taking ownership of their own destiny. In a word, it is a struggle to put power in the hands of the people of God.

This struggle, however, would only be an escape if that empowerment did *not* lead to a sense of mission in the world. If people do not see themselves consecrated as the agents of justice and peace in the world, the kingdom of God remains an abstraction. This requires special reflection within the American Catholic context, especially for the upwardly mobile middle class that forms the greater part of its active membership. A significant majority of American Catholic churchgoers do in fact wield immense power in the world in which they live. They are the active agents of the technological culture that has overtaken the planet.

Yet one of the disappointing features of church renewal is that this fact of church life constantly escapes serious attention. In many of our efforts at renewal, we are creating a para-clergy rather than a community that empowers people to deal with the issues of justice and peace in the context of their own lives and in the midst of their own chosen professions. In the effort to build "community," we often take "involvement in parish functions" as a criterion of "active membership." Where are the zones of reflection, encouragement and modeling where one may be empowered to be a Christian CPA, physician, nurse, social worker, executive secretary, teacher, corporation executive? I have been singularly privileged to spend my adult life in "good" suburban parishes, as well as among Catholics passionately committed to the issues of justice and peace. It is my experience of suburban homilies that they are, like the bedroom communities in which they are uttered, mainly "living room homilies" (The suburban clergy have developed the good sense not to tread verbally in the bedroom any more). They address the narrowly domestic issues or speak of people "on the job" as if they were all simple clerks or powerless minor mechanics. The suburban majority who wield power are never addressed as if they did. It is likewise my experience of many Catholics committed to the causes of justice and peace that, despite rhetoric to the contrary, they define these causes as if they were a part-time preoccupation, an avocation. People's commitments to these issues are all too often measured by the number of committees they belong to, or the number of organized causes that they espouse.

The major moments of the church year hinge around confrontations with corrupted power—Herod and the wise men, the temptation of Jesus, the passion of Christ—yet these things escape the suburban homily as they escape much of the current literature of something called "spirituality." The whole biblical tradition found its first great movement toward being a world religion in a confrontation with corrupt power (Moses before Pharaoh), but we would not know it from what we hear in church or by attending most "parish activities."

When the pope says what he has to say on bedroom morality, the world is all ears. When he says what he has to say on peace and justice (which is considerably more, and not only in terms of quantity), only a select (and usually powerless) few take notice.

If this gaping omission from church life is to be remedied, it will have to be the laity who do it. The loss of the authority to command in the church—which is considerable—has been matched for centuries by a loss of the hierarchy's power to command the sources of power in the world. It had begun to die when the power to excommunicate monarchs no longer had political consequence, and that was a long time ago. In the world in which we live, it is moral authority that counts, if anything counts against the corruption of power. And if the moral authority of the church is to count for anything, then its agents will have to be the laity who stand at the sources of power.

A full enfranchisement of the people of God as agents of God's rule of justice and peace could, in the long run, have everything to do with the recovery and reinterpretation of the traditional Catholic images of God. The traditional images—Mary, the passion of Christ, eucharistic real presence, the pope—have been, but need not be, tied to a model of Christian life seen as submissive obedience to the hierarchy. They could take on new vigor if they were tied instead to a model of the Christian life that appreciated people as empowered for mission in the world. We will now attempt to suggest the lines that reinterpretation might take.

The oldest title of Mary is not, as it is somewhat ineptly translated, "the mother of God," but *Theotokos* (Greek) or *Deipara* (Latin)—the God bearer, the one who bears the living and enfleshed presence of God within the world. It honors her pregnancy as the image of what it means to live as a Christian. If we honor very fallible and imperfect and incomplete human beings as the image of God in the world, the image of pregnancy is in every way appropriate. We do not know fully what the life we carry within and among us will look like when it comes to birth. For a church that must live more in hope than on the splendors of the past, this seems entirely appropriate. And if we can begin to appreciate that the biblical witness portrays Mary not only as a loyal disciple, but also as one who vigorously questions the ways of God and the doings of her son, then there may be some hope of recovering Mary as an image of the feminine in the church, and thus as an image of the feminine face of God.

Catholicism has been a one-sided masculine religion. We need not think only of its traditional patterns of ministry. Its language and mode of action have been strongly military and monarchical. The full enfranchisement of women in the church—to say nothing of the wholeness of men in it—demands that God have a feminine face, as it demands that the life of the church incorporate the feminine fully and wholeheartedly. The exclusion of women from the ministry of the altar (we do not practice it only in terms of priesthood) is not a matter of justice. *Nobody* has a *right* to ordination. It is a matter, rather, of sacramental order, and of finding in our ministers images of holiness and images of the church in its fullness. Officers in the church can only "represent Christ" to the extent that they represent the church. The exclusion of women from office constitutes a significant rejection of the feminine as integral to the life of the church.

The image of the church as the people of God, if taken seriously, calls for an ethic grounded in a sense of responsibility for the poor and oppressed. One of the chief features of God in the biblical tradition is that God is on the side of the poor and oppressed, and if God's people are to be a true image of God's presence in the world, then that is the side they must go to also. The gift of self that this demands obviously finds its model in Christ, who gave himself for the life of the world. The image of God found in the passion could speak vigorously to the kind of suffering that must be endured if there is to be a real identification with the needs of the poor and oppressed. We need not think only of heroic or unusual examples. In the complex technical world in which we live, the important decisions in which power is wielded are always fraught with the particular pain of moral ambiguity and uncertain results. The executive making difficult decisions can be as much a bearer of the cross of Christ as anyone who works more directly and immediately with the dispossessed. Likewise, in a church fraught with the dying pains of an old order, and gripped in the birth pangs of a new one, we need a sturdy appreciation of the church as called to be a bearer of the cross in its own pain of renewal. Confusion, perplexity, poor results, uncertain beginnings, and mistakes are too readily taken as indications that something is "wrong" in the life of the church. We are too ready to ignore the simple fact of all life that most growth involves pain, and indeed that from the Christian perspective, death is the way to resurrection. The mark of authentic "community" is not splendid harmony in which all are in perfect agreement. Rather, it is the capacity of the community of faith to tolerate human weakness and failure and to carry one another's burdens. The suffering Christ was above all a forgiving Christ, and the community that loses this has indeed lost its birthright.

In the sacredness of the bread and wine, we need to see more clearly God's own affirmation of the sacredness of all life. In a technological world, we need to appreciate more fully that bread and wine are the products of human art and skill, the "work of human hands," as the loveliest of our new prayers tells us. And as the ritual has recently made abundantly clear, the fullness of the eucharistic sign is not simply in the bread and wine, but in their being *shared*. The consecration of bread and wine as the "substantial" signs of God's presence in the world places an ultimate value on the goodness of creation, and on the goodness of a creation to be shared with all humankind. To share the eucharistic bread and wine before the altar is an affirmation of an investment in the works of justice and peace, and an affirmation that this investment is not a part-time avocation, but the very stuff of the Christian vocation in the world.

We are beginning to see the emergence of a papacy that is truly universal rather than merely European and Mediterranean. It has done this most effectively in its visits to many nations and peoples, and in its development of a body of teaching on peace and justice unparalleled in any other Christian communion. In a church where co-responsibility becomes more and more a fact of life, and where local initiative is prized (both tendencies which, however slowly, are more and more prized and which are the inevitable result of taking the image of the holiness of the people of God seriously), we need the pope less as an administrator, but much more as a bond of communion among the local churches. As the old European civilization dies, and the new worldwide technological culture more and more replaces it, we need less and less a distinctly "Roman" liturgy that images our God as the God of all. But we do need a liturgy that, however local in its forms of expression, speaks for bonds of communion with other churches across the world. This might emerge less in the shape of the liturgy than in its content: who we pray for may be much more important than the way we pray. All too often, we are so local and parochial in our celebration that the needs of the people of God across the world go unmentioned. And why is it that while pastors would never think of failing to read a letter from the bishop in church, we never hear even a digest of the papal letters to the churches?

In this chapter, we have launched into the realm of the possible rather than the actual. The recovery of the image of the people of God as an effective image to recluster the old and displaced images is a task before us rather than an accomplished fact. Yet, as we have seen, that task is not a mere possibility. It is, rather, a task the church has already taken up, and which has been embraced by the people of God in popular movements, in the raising of new questions, and in the gradual and painful reshaping of church life. We have already begun.

VI

MASS IN A NEW KEY:
THE EUCHARIST AS ACTION
OF THE PEOPLE OF GOD

As we have already seen in previous chapters, the meaning and power of ritual lies not only in the action of performing it, but also in what people understand they are doing when they engage in the ritual. If the celebration of the eucharist seems to "lack a sense of mystery" or "not have a sense of the sacred," it may have as much to do with our own sensibilities about what we are doing as it does with what is done. If we understand the "holy" as what takes place outside the action and the place of the people assembled, we will inevitably define the "holy" as something apart from ourselves, and thus experience something that involves us as being less than "holy." But if we come to a deep appreciation of ourselves as a holy people, we will likewise come to an appreciation of what we do as holy action. Often, the celebration of the eucharist lacks meaning and power for us, not so much because of some inherent defect in the shape of the way we do it, but because of our perceptions of what we are doing.

Our perceptions can be distorted by inadequate use of a rite. As already indicated, many (if not most) church buildings obscure rather than reveal the proper role of the people of God in the liturgy. How many churches are so built that we experience ourselves as gathered together, ministers and people, around the one altar? Do we not, rather, experience ourselves less as participants than as spectators observing an action that takes place before us? Are not most of our churches so arranged that the lay ministers are perceived as "the priest's helpers," instead of priest and ministers together being at our service? Do we not, often, judge and use music on the basis of how it sounds rather than how well it serves our singing with one voice? The almost universal use of leaflet missals in this country dramatizes our self-perception as liturgical consumers rather than liturgical participants. They reflect an understanding of the liturgy as a prepackaged item, because they distract us totally from the event of speaking to and acting with one another, which is the heart of liturgical, and especially, eucharistic prayer. How can I appreciate myself as a member of an assembly of people responsible to one another if I keep my eyes glued to a text in front of me?

But here we have leapt ahead. The issue is one of appreciating ourselves as a holy people, and of appreciating the demands of liturgical prayer in which we are called to full participation as people responsible to one another. Generation upon generation of ritual in which the role of the people was mainly to engage meditatively in ritual has schooled us away from that appreciation. We need a re-schooling of our liturgical perceptions. In this chapter, we will explore the present mass ceremonies and prayers as they offer opportunities for that re-schooling.

If we are going to clarify our perceptions of the mass, we need to ask what we are doing there: what kind of activity is the mass? What is the business of the laity at mass? Most people would readily answer, "to pray," or, if they are thinking of the sermon,[1] "to listen" or "to reflect." None of these answers is at all incorrect, but they may still mask a perception of the role of the people as primarily meditative. As an event of prayer, the mass is an event of prayer *in common,* an event of *liturgical* prayer.

For anyone who has anything like a working Catholic vocabulary, and any experience of the Catholic Church in the last generation, this may sound like a truism. Of course we pray

---

[1] It has become very fashionable to insist that the sermon is to be called a "homily"—the term used in the new official literature. But a homily is simply a sermon in a liturgical context, and it is insufferably churchy to insist that lay people call it anything else.

85

in common. Of course the mass is a liturgy. But what do we mean by prayer? And what do we mean by liturgy? And here, above all, there is a need to clarify our perceptions. Many people will judge a liturgy as "not prayerful" if it does not conform to their presuppositions about what constitutes "real prayer." When the vernacular liturgy was introduced, many people complained that it was "distracting." They were not at all wrong. It was impossible to carry out many of the sorts of devotional activities or exercises in the devout reading of prayers that people could do during the performances of the mass ceremonies of previous generations. The present mass ceremonies and prayers also "interfere" with the effort to make the hour at mass a period of intimate communion between oneself and one's favorite images of God. The current rite of mass is a very awkward space in which to be "alone with God" or "together with Jesus." Also, if one identifies "real prayer" with moods induced by particular sorts of styles and ceremonies (incense and organ music versus, say, guitar music and the use of banners and bright colors), there can be plenty to distract at mass. There is nothing wrong with meditation, with seeking devout interludes "alone with God," or feeling that one has entered the realm of the sacred through particular styles and forms of ceremony. There is also much to recommend such experiences, and they will normally be some part of people's experiences of mass. But such things do not constitute liturgical prayer, and they are certainly not the primary purpose for the church's assembling together to celebrate the eucharist, especially if we take the role of the people as co-celebrants seriously.

To clarify our perceptions, let us begin with some definitions. What does "liturgy" mean? And for that matter, what does it mean to call what we do on Sunday morning "mass" or "eucharist"? It is often said, truly (but not accurately) enough, that the term "liturgy" means "public service." But the important thing about the original meaning of the term is that it is *public service rendered by free and responsible people to and for one another.* It is something we do for one another. Accustomed as we are to perceiving ourselves as lone spectators in a crowd of spectators, this definition seems ill-fitting when we apply it to

86

Sunday mass. Through the rest of this chapter, we will explore how it does (or can and should) fit. For now, let us note that liturgical prayer is not simply speech in common addressed to God. Rather, it is speech to one another addressed in God's "overhearing." We come together because it is important to say things to one another and to God about God and one another. For example, to name ourselves as sinners in church is not only and not primarily to grovel in guilt, but to name ourselves as acceptable to God even though we are sinners, and to call one another to be the kind of people, together and individually, who welcome the sinner.

This may be clearer if we reflect on one of the most ancient names of the mass—eucharist. Eucharist literally means "thanks and praise," but that literal meaning does not get us too far because there are other things we do at mass besides thanking and praising. But the original meaning of the term has to do not only with sentiments of gratitude, awe, wonder, and reverence, but also with the commitment that underlies such sentiments. To give God "thanks and praise" is to *acknowledge* God, to take a stand on the belief that we are graced people who live in a graced world, and to take a stand on living accordingly. The Catholic tradition has consistently named the eucharist "a sacrifice," not because it has to do with giving something up, but because it has to do with taking a stance of commitment before God and before the world. By calling the mass "eucharist," we are saying to one another that God is a good God who has made a good world, and that we understand ourselves as called to sustain or restore or build that good world. By giving thanks over bread broken and cup shared, and, by naming these as the body and blood of Christ, we are saying that we stake our lives on a vocation to put the unity and well-being of the human family above every other value.

Our name for the eucharist, "mass," is simply English for the Latin *missa,* which literally means "sending." Older Catholics will remember that the mass ended with the dismissal, *Ite missa est,* tragically mistranslated "Go, the mass is ended." It actually means "Go, because you are sent," and is a play on the double use of the term for both the Christian vocation in the world and for the action of the eucharist. That ancient name, *missa,* has everything to do with the older term *"eucharistia"* or eucharist. For what we come together to do is to trace the shape of the Christian vocation in the world in sacramental action. We name ourselves as an assembly of forgiven and forgiving people, as active hearers of God's word, as people concerned for others, as grateful sharers of God's gifts.

Here, a word needs to be said about sacramental action. Accustomed as we are to thinking of the consecrated wafer as the "Blessed Sacrament," or of sacraments generally as special sacred ceremonies "done" to individuals, we miss much of the wider and deeper meaning of sacraments generally, and of the eucharist in particular. In its fullness, the "holy sacrament of the eucharist" is not simply the sacred host (consecrated bread), but the full action of the eucharist, from beginning to end. This is why the official teaching of the church insists that Christ is really present in the assembly gathered, in the proclaiming of the word, and in the ministers, as well as under the forms of bread and wine. Sacraments are not simply what the priest does, or what individuals receive, but what the whole church does. And understood from this angle, sacraments "happen" not simply for the sake of individuals, nor even simply for the sake of the church, but for the sake of the world. They are what classical theology called "signs" (not as in neon signs but as thunder is the sign of a storm, or leaves a sign of spring), which means they are manifestations of faith that act out what God intends for the world. To consecrate and share bread and wine with words about death and resurrection and covenant and sacrifice is to affirm that God hallows all human caring and sharing, that the life of Jesus was poured out to hallow these, and that we commit ourselves to sharing that life.

This applies to all the sacraments, not just to the eucharist. To baptize a baby is a "sign" of hope for all babies born into the world, as the anointing of the sick is to affirm both meaning in human suffering and a commitment to the arts of healing and reconciliation. This dimension of sacrament as sign may be much obscured in practice, but no Catholicity worth the name denies it. And anything less than this classical perspective leaves us open to perceiving the sacraments as magical medicine.

An understanding of sacraments as "signs" also frees us to deal creatively with the tension between what we *say* we are about at the liturgy and what we actually *are*, as we experience ourselves. As signs, the sacraments are actions that speak for what we hope, as well as for what we are here and now. Most of the gestures identified by older people as "new" in the mass—the exchange of peace greetings, the sharing of the cup, the taking of communion in the hand (they are actually contemporary versions of very ancient practices)—are gestures of sharing. They inevitably raise questions about the shared life of the community that assembles for the eucharist. What does it mean that strangers and semi-strangers worship together and use these gestures? Certainly it calls into question a style of parish life and liturgical celebration that does not involve people with one another. At the same time the gestures may seem hollow if they do not connect with a sense of church life that is as vigorously participatory as the liturgy. How can we share the cup of Christ's blood if we are not called to share one another's burdens? How can we offer one another the peace if we do not experience ourselves as belonging to a community of faith that invites us to peace with one another? How can we touch the body of Christ from the altar if we are unwilling to be touched by the wounds in the body of Christ that stands before that altar? There is a challenge here to parish life as it is often lived.

But at the same time, as signs of hope, these same gestures of caring and sharing (rooted firmly in the oldest and best of our liturgical tradition) are actions that express what we hope for and what we commit ourselves to. Theology calls them "sacramental signs of the kingdom of God," which means that they are ritual actions that speak for our deepest values and hopes, and not simply for ourselves "as we are." Insofar as we are less than a whole community of faith at prayer, insofar as we find the liturgical gestures less than an accurate manifestation of the life of the parish community, we are expressing a hope that remains yet to be fulfilled. There is nothing "dishonest" with sharing the cup with strangers or exchanging the peace with them. In the ritual event of sharing with unknown neighbors, we are pledging ourselves to building a world (however slowly, painfully, and partially) where all become neighbors.

One of the lovely (and very useful) words that has disappeared from our working Catholic vocabulary is *devotion*, mainly because we associate it with the "devotions" of a bygone age, and because we associate it with styles of prayer that have gone out of fashion. We have also lost the word because it has often come to mean the creating of a particular sort of pious mood that is normally impossible to sustain at a contemporary eucharist. Devotion, however, really has little to do either with special moods or styles of prayer, and has everything to do with the quality of what we do. We speak of people, for instance, who are devoted to one another. By that we mean their willingness to see one another through good times and bad, their willingness both to rejoice in and bear with one another. To participate in the eucharist with devotion is not a matter of having a capacity for particular moods or a penchant for particular gestures, but of committing oneself consistently to the values for which the eucharistic action speaks. The warm handclasp of one's pew partner is as "devotional" as kissing a relic (more so, in fact), provided that we understand that what we are doing together is making promises about our faith. We are committing ourselves to being the agents of the peace of Christ in the world.

The Latin word from which we derive our English word "devotion" means "to make promises," and this is a good way of describing what our "public service" (i.e., service to one another) in the liturgy is: we are making promises in faith. We are saying to one another what we believe life is all about at its very heart, and pledging ourselves to live by what we believe. We are not merely saying this in words, but also performing it in action, above all the actions of presenting and sharing together bread and wine while naming them as the body and blood of Christ, the bread of life and the cup of salvation. We call upon God as the giver of all good gifts, claim that the inner nature of God is most fully revealed in the Christ who gave his life for others, and acknowledge ourselves as called to share the life of that good God, not only with one another, but also with the world.

90

The character of the eucharist as an action by which we make promises to one another is the reason for the constant references to both God's covenant with God's people and to the Holy Spirit that appear in our new prayers. "Covenant" is another word for "promise," and it refers both to the fact that God is pledged to us, and that we are pledged to God through our pledge in faith to one another. And the Holy Spirit is the Spirit of promise, not only because the Spirit was promised by Christ, but also because God's promise and ours only unfold by the work of the Spirit. In making our promises to one another, we are not gritting our teeth to pull ourselves up by our spiritual bootstraps. We are giving ourselves to the unfolding of the work of the Spirit in the world.

The nature of the eucharist as an affirmation of our promises in faith to one another should serve to clarify the relationship between what an older generation called outward ceremonial and inner disposition. To be preoccupied with "style" in liturgy distorts its meaning. The current cafeteria of "quiet," "high," and "folk" liturgies offered by many parishes may well reflect a consumerist approach to worship that ignores or at least underplays the sacramental nature of eucharist, which calls us into a unity that transcends, among other things, differences in taste. At the same time, if we are making promises to one another by what we say and do together, how we say and do it cannot be a matter of sheer indifference. People need singable hymns, audible words, preaching that touches their lives, ministries that both speak for and call them to a sense of serving one another at the liturgy. These are the right of Christian people, not additional decorative luxuries. And Christians have the right and duty to seek them out.

The nature of the eucharist as an affirmation of our promises in faith to one another should also serve to clarify perceptions about what constitutes "devout attention," i.e., attention with devotion. As long as the congregation was placed in the role of spectator, devout attention could only mean "following along" the ceremonies in the sanctuary, either by some meditative device or by reading the prayers to oneself while they were being said in Latin at the altar. But if the liturgy is a speaking and acting of promises to one another, then the sight and sound of the congregation are as important to our prayer as the sight and sound of the priest.

It is difficult to understand how this sort of attention can be served by gluing our noses to leaflet missals while the priest is uttering prayers in our name (all of the prayers are) or when a reader is proclaiming the word. The prayers and readings are naming us as part of the people of God, and if we shut out the people of God around us from view, we are reducing the notion to a comfortable abstraction. We are effectually distracting ourselves from the very business for which we are gathered. "God's people" are not fictitious early Christians in togas or imaginary Israelites in burnouses or riding camels. God's people are Mrs. McGillicuddy with her divorce, Mr. Plodowski with his raspy voice, the usher in highwaters, the child thumping the pew, and the new people bringing down the neighborhood.

An older generation was schooled to screen out "distractions" from prayer, meaning especially those distractions constituted by the sight and sound of other people. That schooling has left us with a significant segment of the Catholic population assuming that when we are at the liturgy, our business is to rivet our attention as securely on the liturgical text as we can, whether that be the text as spoken by the priest or other ministers, or the text as it appears on the printed page of the leaflet missal. Part of the mania for textual variety in prayers may be rooted in the assumption that it is our business to take in every word of the text every time we are at the liturgy. This is to misunderstand the nature of liturgical action as public service and as promises to one another. Promise formulas are notoriously repetitive, and in fact, the more important they are, the more repetitive they are. They are also dramatic rather than poetic. That is to say, the point is not so much to hang on every word as to use them in such a way that they can be used again and again within the context of a ritual action that speaks for the coming together of God and our lives. We are not supposed to hang onto the text, but to hang the text onto our lives, and our lives onto the text. Thus a certain mental "floating" between the texts we hear proclaimed and our private thoughts (however "profane") is a nor-

92

mal part of authentic liturgical prayer. Devout attention has more to do with the attitudes we bring to liturgical prayer than it does with the vagaries of our imaginations.

The Order of Mass

Traditional commentaries on the mass for lay people have usually given a ceremony-by-ceremony description of what happens in the sanctuary, explaining what those ceremonies "mean." This was useful as long as the role of the people was, for all practical purposes, to simply kneel in their places and meditate on what the priest was doing at the altar. Unfortunately, this approach perpetuated and reinforced the notion that the mass was akin to a play to be watched, unfolding act by act. Now that the mass ceremonies have been considerably simplified, there is no need to "explain" many of them. If a minister lifts a book, it simply means what is obvious—that he is about to carry it to the place where it will be used. There is also no need to "explain" what are best described as family etiquette and manners—certain forms of reverence (bows, genuflections, etc.). They all simply mean that we take seriously what we are doing, as any etiquette does. There are, of course, a few family relics in our etiquette—the mixing in the chalice of wine and water, for instance, or the washing of the priest's hands. You can strain for some mystical meaning in these little relics, but the more obvious significance is that, as a historic family of faith, we have our own odd little ways of doing things, as all old families do. And we keep doing them simply because we always have as long as anyone can remember. Those little family manners were in place long before medieval commentators attached a mystical meaning to them, and the fact is that they simply mean that we have been celebrating the mass for a very long time.

The same is true of the various ministries in the present order of mass. The "meaning" of the priest's ministry, obviously, is that the priest presides over the assembly; readers read, servers serve, and so on. Unless one is going to take on one of those ministries as a service to the assembly, one needs no special commentary on those roles: their meaning is manifest in what they do.

What really cries out for commentary is the people's role, for it is vastly misunderstood. Most of the idiosyncrasies that have invaded our worship in recent years are the result of that misunderstanding. In this commentary, then, we will concentrate on that role. The basic question is—what does it mean that we do the things we do in church?

We will begin with the eucharistic prayer. This is not at all an obvious starting point if you view the eucharist as a play that unfolds in several acts. It is, however, an obvious starting point if you take seriously the assertion of the General Instruction of the Roman Missal that the eucharistic prayer is the "center and high point of the entire celebration" (No. 54). This is not the way we tend to experience the eucharistic action as it actually unfolds. But much of the way we experience the eucharist has to do with the perceptions we bring to it. Here, we will attempt to clarify those perceptions.

The first of those perceptions that needs clarifying is the notion that the eucharist is a play that unfolds in several acts, one of which is the eucharistic prayer. The eucharist *is* a dramatic action, but it is a ritual action, not a theatrical one. What is done in church and what is done in theaters naturally have much in common in terms of their forms and patterns, because they are both dramatic actions. But a play is a play and a ritual is a ritual. And the eucharistic prayer has the special function of articulating what the *whole* of the ritual action is about: it voices what it means to gather (ritualized in the introductory rites), tell our story (ritualized in the liturgy of the word), take bread and wine (ritualized in the preparation of the altar and gifts), and share them (ritualized in the holy communion). Instead of imagining the various gestures and ceremonies of the mass as a play that unfolds before our eyes, imagine it instead as a set of actions that are formalized so that they can be carried out by a large gathering of people, with the eucharistic prayer as a great verbal canopy or umbrella that shadows those actions and voices their meaning.

For older readers, it may be helpful to note that, properly speaking, the eucharistic prayer includes the dialogue between priest and people that precedes the prayer, the beginning of the prayer, known as the Preface, and the part that used to be identified as the Canon—the part that follows the sanctus (holy, holy, holy Lord) and extends to the great amen (the amen after the doxology, "Through him, with him, and in him . . . etc.).

Both the former custom of having the priest recite most of the prayer silently and the present custom of having the congregation kneel after the sanctus have tended to obscure the nature of the prayer as speaking for the whole assembly. We tend to identify this prayer as the "priest's prayer" par excellence, whereas it is the priest's prayer precisely because it belongs to the people: the priest is speaking on our behalf and in our name. This prayer sums up the whole meaning of the eucharistic action—not just the meaning of the moment of its utterance, but the meaning of all that goes before and the meaning of what happens afterwards. As the General Instruction of the Roman Missal asserts, "The meaning of the prayer is that the *whole congregation* offers the sacrifice" (No. 54). This is why the acclamations of the eucharistic prayer are so important: through them we take ownership of the prayer and affirm it as our own.

So first a word about acclamation is in order. What on earth is an acclamation, and why do we apply this term to the responses we make to the priest in the dialogue before the prayer, or to responses like the sanctus or great amen? The comparison is often made with cheers in sports arenas. But the comparison is not entirely appropriate, and not only because liturgy is (or should be) a more serious business than sport. The comparison is not appropriate because cheers are appropriate to spectators, and as we have more than suggested, the proper role of the laity in liturgy is not that of spectators, but that of co-celebrants. The priest is at the altar because we are there, not the other way around. Acclamation is a *political* rather than an athletic activity: it is the affirmation by the enfranchised that they share in a decision. We speak, for instance, of people being elected by acclamation, and we mean that the assembly speaks with one voice to declare its assent. Normally, that is done with full vigor (our ancestors in faith shouted the great amen). The reduction of acclamations to mere recitation, or to the syrupy and bouncy, boppy stuff that often passes for liturgical music, sadly trivializes the weighty role of the assembly at prayer. Good acclamations would be full, robust, vigorous, and dignified. The sacred role of the laity in the eucharistic prayer demands no less.

That role of the people is especially marked out in the dialogue before the prayer: the priest only prays in our name when he has secured the attention and assent of the people in the dialogue. The abandonment of chant during this solemn dialogue is unfortunate: it tends to reduce the prayer to one more segment of the celebration, on a par with any other. By the same token, of course, the use of any sort of musical style that leaves the congregation with a sense that the acclamations are not fully theirs is a liturgical distortion. It deprives the laity of their rights as co-celebrants.

If the best way to understand the ceremonies of the mass is to jump into the center and explore the eucharistic prayer, the best way to understand the eucharistic prayer is to jump into *its* center and clarify our understanding of the institution narrative (the story of the last supper, commonly known as the "consecration"). Part of the reason for perceiving the eucharistic prayer as exclusively the priest's prayer is that we have tended to perceive the eucharistic prayer as simply a framework for the institution narrative, understood simply as "words of consecration." That perception was reinforced by the ringing of bells and the dramatic elevation of the host (consecrated wafer) and chalice as ceremonial accompaniments to the priest's recital of the narrative, practices introduced only in the high middle ages. Piety looked to this moment as the high point of the eucharistic liturgy when Christ became present under the forms of bread and wine. Contemporary studies have stressed the point that the whole eucharistic prayer is a prayer of consecration. The General Instruction of the Roman Missal describes the whole prayer as a prayer of "thanksgiving and sanctification." It describes the citation of the last supper as "institution narrative *or* consecration." The suggestion is that the narrative is more than *simply* "words of consecration."

The narrative is embedded in the whole prayer to sum up the meaning of the prayer, and thus to sum up the meaning of the whole eucharistic action. In other words, the narrative speaks not only for what the priest is doing at the altar, but for the meaning of what all of us are doing when we gather for eucharist.

In this dramatic narrative, where the priest speaks "in the person of Christ," the assembly is identified in that action with Christ's disciples. We are there as hearers of the command to "do this in memory of me." For Christ is described as being at supper with his friends (all of them, not just the apostles), and the command is not simply to say words over bread and wine, but to *do* certain things—take bread and wine in thanks and praise, and share them with one another. These actions constitute the "memory" of Jesus. We are conditioned not to hear the reference to the disciples as including ourselves, especially by representations of the last supper that include only the twelve apostles—no women, no very young people, no very old people, and no diversity of social condition. In terms of the New Testament background of this narrative, we would be more faithful to the original accounts if we were to picture Mary the mother of Jesus, Martha and Mary, Lazarus, Joseph of Arimathea and a host of other friends of Jesus from the area around Jerusalem as present at the last supper. The upper room of the last supper stories is also the upper room of Pentecost day, and there St. Luke quietly reminds us, "And Mary the mother of Jesus was there" (Acts 1:14).

What, then, is the "this" that we are doing, and what does it mean to do it "in memory" of Jesus? "This," as we have already noted, is not simply the business of consecrating the bread and wine, but the action of taking bread and wine in thanks and praise and sharing them with one another. It refers to the presentation of the gifts of bread and wine (commonly called the offertory but named officially as the "Preparation of the Altar and Gifts"). This is the action of "taking." The thanks and praise refer to the eucharistic prayer, and to our sharing in it. Obviously, the eating and drinking refer to the ritual we call the communion.

But Jesus is cited as having us do "this" as an action "in memory" of him. The Latin *commemoratio*, which our translators render "memory," is itself a translation of a New Testament Greek expression *eis anamnesin* which is only weakly

97

translated as "in memory." It is weakly translated because there really is no effective English equivalent. If we are to take hold of the meaning of Jesus' command to us—to do the eucharistic actions "in memory" of him—we need to have some sense of what a memorial action means. It is much more than "looking back" to the last supper. We can note this in the very texts of our own prayers. After the priest says "Do this in memory of me," we are invited to join in the "memorial acclamation"— "Christ has died, Christ is risen, Christ will come again"; or "When we eat this bread and drink this cup, we proclaim your death, Lord Jesus, until you come in glory"; or "Dying you destroyed our death, rising you restored our life. Lord Jesus, come in glory"; or "Lord, by your cross and resurrection you have set us free. You are the Savior of the world."

The priest then goes on to speak in our name, speaking not of the last supper, but of Christ's death and resurrection, and saying "We offer you in thanksgiving this holy and living sacrifice," or some other variant of the offering language cited here from Eucharistic Prayer III. The "this," then, of the "do this in memory of me," is the actions of taking, thanking, praising, and sharing bread and cup. But those actions are done "in memory" of Jesus' death and resurrection, and they constitute a "holy and living sacrifice." The section of the eucharistic prayer (technically know as the anamnesis) that immediately follows the institution narrative is in fact an interpretation of the words of Jesus, "Do this in memory of me." So is the memorial acclamation. Some (myself included) believe that the memorial acclamation would better follow the anamnesis so that the connection between the narrative and the anamnesis would be clearer to people.

The issue is somewhat confused here because we have been prone to pose a false dilemma: is the eucharist a meal or a sacrifice? The correct answer is yes. It is a meal with a sacrificial meaning. Sacrifice refers not to what is performed in outward act, but to what the act means. And it does not mean killing. Christ's death was sacrificial, not because he was killed, but because in dying and rising he reconciled us to God. The eucharist is a sacrifice, not because for a long period in our history we adopted the paraphernalia of temple cult (vesture, stone altars, a focus on a language and iconography of death and bloodshed), but because it is the ritual action by which we celebrate our reconciliation to God. St. Paul exhorts us to "offer ourselves as a living sacrifice," and he is not exhorting us to get killed, but to live a life of hospitality and concern for others after the model of Jesus who gave himself for sinners (Cf. Romans 13). In the first place, then, "Do this in memory of me" means: "Take bread and wine, give praise and thanksgiving, and share the bread and wine. When you do this, you are sharing the very sacrifice that gives life to the world." This is what the catechism meant when it described the eucharist as the "unbloody sacrifice of Calvary." And this is the meaning of the words "This is my body . . . this is my blood." It is not that the sacramental forms of bread and wine somehow create a culinary time tunnel back to Calvary, but that by sharing the consecrated bread and wine we are nourished by the Christ who died and rose for us.

The nature of the eucharist as a ritual meal with a sacrificial meaning is best understood when we realize that in the New Testament, the last supper stories simply represent a concentrated account of what the whole ministry of Jesus was understood to be about. We have tended to see the last supper stories as accounts of how Jesus taught the apostles to function as priests. We have lost the intimate connection between the last supper stories and the other supper stories of Jesus' ministry (including the resurrection meal stories). For the New Testament authors, Jesus' meals with sinners and outcasts, where he welcomes them and transforms their lives, are the hallmark of his ministry. The "last" supper, embedded in the story of his laying down his life for us, marks that welcoming, feeding, and transforming of the sinner as the very heart of his ministry. It is the "last" in the sense of "ultimate." This is why Jesus' words over the cup refer to the "new and everlasting covenant" which is "for the remission of sins." We meet the Christ who welcomes the sinner. And in telling his disciples, "Do this in memory of me," Jesus was not simply commanding the repetition of a ritual. They already knew the ritual: it was the ritual of the Jewish festal meal. It is "in memory" of Jesus because what the church does when it gathers is to name itself as a community of welcome, forgiveness, and transformation, in union with the Christ who came to reconcile the world with God. To say amen to the eucharistic prayer is not simply to assent to Christ's having been made present on the altar, but to identify ourselves as forgiven sinners called to be a community of welcome, forgiveness, and transformation. This is what *The Roman Missal* means when it says that the prayer's meaning is that the "whole congregation offers the sacrifice." Acclaiming the eucharistic prayer is in the nature of a solemn vow. The sacrifice we offer is a commitment to a life shaped and transformed by care for others.

This is acted out ritually in the gestures of the laity that precede and follow the eucharistic prayer—the collection at the preparation of the altar and gifts that precedes, and the saying of the Lord's Prayer and the exchange of peace that follow the eucharistic prayer. The conjunction of the collection with the "taking" of the bread and wine at the altar is neither a mere convenience nor an "intrusion of the secular."[2] It is in fact a sacred act *because* it connects the ritual of "taking" the bread and wine with the secular. By presenting money along with bread and wine, we are affirming that the bread and wine represent the very stuff of our lives ("work of human hands," as our prayers have it), entwined with our hopes and dreams and cares, our ideals and our struggles. We are saying in a gesture that the sacrifice we offer is a commitment to a life shaped and transformed by care for others.

The tradition of having the Lord's Prayer follow after the eucharistic prayer, as a kind of "bridge" to the actions of the communion, underscores the character of the acclamation of the eucharistic prayer as an uttering of a solemn vow to one another. The Lord's Prayer is an extended acclamation of the eucharistic prayer (which is why it should never be co-opted by a choir). To name God as "Our Father" is not to name God as a male parent, but to identify with the Jesus who called God "Father" (and what

---

[2]One wonders how Christians, who claim to believe that the center of their faith is the Incarnation, can make such nonsensical statements.

he meant by "Father" is that God is a God who welcomes the sinner, the poor, and the outcast), and to pray for the shaping of the world as he would have it. As the Lord's Prayer is used in the eucharistic liturgy, it centers on the line "forgive us our trespasses as we forgive those who trespass against us"—a point made clear by the prayerful commentary of the priest that follows:

> Deliver us, Lord, from every evil, and grant us peace in our day. In your mercy keep us free from sin and protect us from all anxiety as we wait in joyful hope for the coming of our Savior, Jesus Christ.

It is a prayer to be a community that believes and trusts in the mercy of God, and lives by it.

The words of the prayers are underscored by a gesture: the exchange of peace following the Lord's Prayer. By turning to our neighbor, we are called to acknowledge that carrying the Lord's peace is no simple or easy task. It is a peace we are called to share, not keep in our hearts.

To "Do this in memory of me," then, is (to make an understatement) a serious business, for we are committing ourselves to live as Jesus lived. At the same time, this is not to be understood as saying that we are a community of the pure and the perfect. The altar of sacrifice, as we have already noted, is at the same time a table of welcome, and we gather as a community of sinners. The sinners to be welcomed are not just some others outside, but ourselves as well. This is abundantly clear not only from experience, but also from the New Testament stories of Jesus at table. Both Judas and Peter shared the last supper, and we know their record as disciples. And we have no business saying, "Yes, but that was before the resurrection." The story of Peter's betraying Jesus three times was kept alive among the new churches because in many ways he went right on betraying Jesus afterwards. Read the tenth chapter of the Acts of the Apostles for another variant on Peter's betrayal, and St. Paul's account of Peter's performance in the second chapter of the Epistle to the Galatians.

The nature of the eucharistic action—as a sharing of a table of welcome, as well as an altar of sacrifice—is voiced in the

eucharistic prayer through its dual character as prayer of praise
and thanksgiving, and of petition. We begin by praising and
thanking God. This culminates in the sanctus but often extends
into the first part of the prayer after the sanctus as in Prayers
III and IV:

Prayer III

Father, you are holy indeed,
and all creation rightly gives you
    praise.
All life, all holiness comes from you
through your Son, Jesus Christ our
    Lord,
by the working of the Holy Spirit.
From age to age you gather a people
    to yourself,
so that from east to west
a perfect offering may be made
to the glory of your name.

Prayer IV

Father, we acknowledge your
    greatness:
all your actions show your wisdom
    and love.
You formed man in your own
    likeness
and set him over the whole world
to serve you, his creator,
and to rule over all creatures.
Even when he disobeyed you and
    lost your friendship
you did not abandon him to the
    power of death,
but helped all men to seek and
    find you.
Again and again you offered a
    covenant to man,
and through the prophets taught him
    to hope for salvation.
Father, you so loved the world
that in the fullness of time you sent
    your only Son to be our Savior.
He was conceived through the power
    of the Holy Spirit,

and born of the Virgin Mary,
a man like us in all things but sin.
To the poor he proclaimed the good
   news of salvation,
to prisoners, freedom,
and to those in sorrow, joy.
In fulfillment of your will
he gave himself up to death;
but by rising from the dead,
he destroyed death and restored life.
And that we might live no longer for
   ourselves but for him,
he sent the Holy Spirit from you,
   Father,
as his first gift to those who believe,
to complete his work on earth
and bring us the fullness of grace.

In this giving of thanks and praise (Preface, sanctus, and, in the case of the prayers cited above, post-sanctus), we identify ourselves as a graced community—as called by God to be God's people, as saved and transformed through Christ in the Spirit. This is the fundamental spirit of the prayer, and it gives the eucharist its very name. All eucharistic prayers return to that basic note of praise and thanksgiving in the concluding doxology ("Through him, with him, and in him . . ."). This is the ground of our ability to offer our lives in sacrifice: we name ourselves as blessed by the mercy of God, a people acceptable to him. The core of Jesus' teaching about God as "Father" was God's creative receptivity: that the heart of God is love and mercy. Only to the extent that we experience ourselves as acceptable people can we turn to others in love and acceptance. But this is the work of a lifetime: indeed, it is the unachieved task of human history.

To the praise and thanksgiving, then, the eucharistic prayer adds petition for what remains unfinished in our lives. The priest has no sooner spoken for our offering the eucharist in praise and thanksgiving than he begins to pray for the full accomplishment of the sacrifice of Christ in our lives:

Prayer I
we offer to you, God of glory and

majesty,
this holy and perfect sacrifice:
the bread of life
and the cup of eternal salvation.

Look with favor on these offerings
and accept them as once you accepted
the gifts of your servant Abel,
the sacrifice of Abraham, our father
    in faith,
and the bread and wine offered by
    your priest Melchisedech.

Almighty God,
we pray that your angel may take this
    sacrifice
to your altar in heaven.
Then, as we receive from this altar
the sacred body and blood of your Son,
let us be filled with every grace and blessing.

Prayer II
we offer you, Father, this life-giving
    bread,
this saving cup.
We thank you for counting us worthy
to stand in your presence and serve
    you.
May all of us who share in the body
    and blood of Christ
be brought together in unity by the
    Holy Spirit.

Prayer III
we offer you in thanksgiving this
    holy and living sacrifice.

Look with favor on your Church's
    offering,
and see the Victim whose death has
    reconciled us to yourself.
Grant that we, who are nourished by
    his body and blood,
may be filled with his Holy Spirit,

104

and become one body, one spirit in
 Christ.

May he make us an everlasting gift
 to you,
and enable us to share in the
 inheritance of your saints.

Prayer IV
we offer you his body and blood,
the acceptable sacrifice
which brings salvation to the whole
 world.

Lord, look upon this sacrifice which
 you have given to your Church;
and by your Holy Spirit, gather all
 who share this bread and wine
into the one body of Christ, a living
 sacrifice of praise.

In the newer prayers (II, III, and IV), the bond between the
part of the prayer that gives praise and thanks and the part that
petitions for the full accomplishment of God's work in us is
underscored by invoking the work of the Spirit. The same Spirit
who has begun to work in the world and in us is the Spirit of
promise who will bring God's work to completion. For the same
reason, in the newer prayers, the remembrance of the saints quickly follows the invocation of the Spirit. The saints are a promise
that what God's Spirit has begun, God's Spirit will complete.
In the newer prayers, too, the prayer for the fulfillment of Christ's
sacrifice in us, the invocation of the Spirit, and the remembrance
of the saints, are bound up with prayers for the church, the hierarchy, and the dead. There are only passing references to those outside the household of faith: "bring them (i.e., departed believers)
and all the departed into the light of your presence" (Prayer II);
"In mercy and love unite all your children wherever they may
be" (Prayer III); "Remember . . . all who seek you with a sincere
heart" (Prayer IV). With such minimal reference to others, such
prayers may seem unutterably churchy (a criticism I myself have
made), and they may appear to be duplicative of the prayer of

the faithful (general intercessions). But this is to misunderstand the somewhat different character of the prayer of the faithful (a point to be explored shortly). In the eucharistic prayer we pray especially for the hierarchy and the faithful departed, as well as for the rest of the church scattered throughout the world, because we are naming ourselves as a community of sinners. We are owning up to the incompleteness of God's work in God's own household. And we are entrusting that, too, to the unfailing mercy of God.

If we take the eucharistic prayer as the "center and high point" of the eucharistic celebration and take seriously the assertion of *The Roman Missal* that the meaning of the prayer is that "the whole congregation offers the sacrifice, then we are in a much better position to understand the two segments of the eucharistic liturgy that are strongly "penitential"—the customary beginning of mass[3] with some expression of penitence after the priest's greeting, and the language of the communion rite. Taken out of context, the expressions "Lord, have mercy," "I confess . . ." "Lamb of God . . . have mercy on us," "Lord, I am not worthy to receive you . . . , " can only sound like abject admissions of guilt, no more than repeated pleas for pardon. Coming as they do at such critical points in the liturgy, almost at its very beginning and immediately prior to the communion, they seem to define the laity simply as a pack of guilty sinners and the purpose of the eucharist as inducing a sense of unworthiness. Certain musical interpretations of these rites (or the lack thereof) only reinforce such impressions. The impression is also reinforced by the unfortunate suggested (not required) alternative to the priest's introduction to the penitential rites: "In order to prepare to celebrate the sacred mysteries, let us call to mind our sins." This is heard as an invitation to an examination of conscience, a "quick feast of sins," as one poet has it. And in their liturgical ignorance, a number of publishers of leaflet missals have pro-

---

[3]In certain masses, e.g., those for special groups, and for certain special occasions, e.g., baptisms, funerals, and weddings, the "penitential rites" at the beginning are omitted, at least if the official norms are taken seriously.

moted invitations to the "Lord, have mercy" litany which begin, "For the times we have . . . Lord, have mercy." The Latin original of that alternative introduction does not bid us to "call to mind our sins." Its operative verb is *agnoscamus*—"let us acknowledge our sins."

The point of all the penitential expressions is not to drive us inward into a review of our sins, but outward into an acknowledgment that we stand before a merciful God. Both the beginning of mass and the beginning of the communion rite itself are filled with "penitential" expressions, but their tone is one of gratitude, not of groveling. The Greek and Latin originals of the "Lord, have mercy" and "Lamb of God" and "Lord, I am not worthy" all carry the sense that God and his Christ are merciful. "Lord, have mercy" means "Lord, you have mercy," not simply "Lord, please grant mercy." By owning up to our sinfulness in the midst of the assembly of God's people (who, in traditional language, "represent Christ": this is the meaning of the official teaching that Christ is present in the assembly), we are acknowledging, in the first place, that this is a place where it is safe to own up to that sinfulness. We are acknowledging God as a merciful God. We are also calling one another to be a community of mercy, a place where the sinner and the broken find welcome. And in the acknowledgment that this is a safe place to own up to our sinfulness, we are making a commitment to live a merciful life ourselves.

With many hundreds of years behind us of a liturgical language not understood by the people, we need to keep in mind that after twenty years of the use of our own language in church, we are still babies at knowing how to use it well. Liturgical language, like all language about God, is "odd": it has its own rules of discourse that are not like those of any other sort of discourse. And the language of liturgy only makes sense when it is set against the ritual context within which it is used. If we "acknowledge our sins" in order to "prepare to celebrate the sacred mysteries," it is not because we have to come shamefaced before the Lord's table. And in saying "Lord, I am not worthy," we are not saying "Thanks, but no thanks, I don't belong here." Our marching up to communion right after that belies this interpretation. Confessions of sinfulness in church, measured against what we actually do, which is to share in the Lord's table, are confessions of God's merciful love revealed in Christ. It is a matter of saying that we accept the altar of sacrifice as a table of welcome, and that in offering the sacrifice of our own lives at that altar, we are simply pledging ourselves to welcome, heal, and nourish others as we have been welcomed, healed, and nourished. In between, we are accepting that we do that in the context of a community of disciples as ragged and imperfect and shortsighted as ourselves. And we are praying that the mercy we have already known in our lives will continue to be there.

Previously, I suggested that we should think of the eucharistic prayer as a great umbrella or canopy over the whole celebration of the eucharist. We can also think of it as a great sound center that sends reverberations into the other prayers of the mass, especially the shorter acclamations and responses of the people. In their ritual context, "I confess . . . , " "Lord, have mercy," "Lamb of God . . . ," "Lord, I am not worthy . . . ," echo the praise and thanksgiving and petition for fulfillment of the eucharistic prayer. They are small ways of acknowledging God's mercy, and by acknowledging it, committing ourselves to live in hope and love, and by so doing, taking our part in the sacrifice acceptable to God, which is to do justice and to love mercy.

We have not yet said anything about the liturgy of the word. And by placing commentary on it after the commentary on the eucharistic prayer and, by extension, the holy communion, I have suggested a certain subordination of the liturgy of the word to the liturgy of the eucharist (the official name for preparation of the altar and gifts, eucharistic prayer, and holy communion). In the Catholic tradition, the eucharistic celebration is the proclamation of the gospel *par excellence:* to celebrate the eucharist is to enact the gospel of Jesus Christ. In our commentary on the eucharistic prayer, we have explored why that is so. We are not about the performance of a cult somehow separated from the church's mission in the world or from the lives of its members. Rather, we come together around the altar table to affirm that we do indeed acknowledge Jesus Christ as God's good news, and we act out what that good news is about as a people called by

108

the mercy of God to live that mercy in the world. By our amen to the eucharistic sacrifice, we accept our call to live the gospel in the world.

At the same time, the liturgy of the word is not a mere preliminary to the liturgy of the eucharist. What is proclaimed in the readings is summed up in the eucharistic prayer (hence certain festal, seasonal, and occasional variations in the prayer). Good preaching will call us to an ever deeper appreciation of what it means to stand before the altar and utter our vows and promises to one another in the action we call eucharist. Indeed, the more we understand the eucharist as connected with the life we live, the more the proclamation of the word will be experienced as a necessity of the life of faith. These things scarcely need to be said. Current complaints about homilies not touching "real life" reflect the instinct of authentic faith for the real meaning of the liturgy of the word.

In many ways, the liturgy of the word defies commentary here because much of it consists of the readings from the scriptures, and they simply "mean" what they say. It is the task of Bible study, meditation, and preaching to wrestle with those texts, not the task of liturgical commentary.

We do, however, need a clearer perception of the people's role in the liturgy of the word, which is not one simply of listeners but also one of proclaimers. The readings from scripture are embedded in a ritual pattern that identifies the people as actively engaged in the business of proclaiming the word. Notice, first of all, that the liturgy of the word opens with lay people reading the first two passages of scripture. And if there is a deacon, the deacon is supposed to read the gospel, even if the pope himself is presiding. Likewise, the people join in the "responsorial psalm" (somewhat unhelpfully named, because it is less a simple "response" than a way of engaging the people in proclaiming the word as a body). In other words, every ministry of the church, including the ministry of the people, is ritually engaged in the business of proclaiming the word. We are accepting a responsibility as active hearers.

Notice, too, that every reading begins with a notation on authorship: "A reading from the book of . . . "; "A reading from the letter of St. Paul to . . . . "; "A reading from the gospel according to . . . . " And we use not one, but, on Sunday, three readings, three readings from three different authors to three very different communities of faith very different from our own. Taken seriously, this is a call to a reflective engagement with the text that is anything but passive. We are not getting the word of God "neat," but as it is filtered through particular authors for other times and other places, and the burden is placed on us to find the word of God for ourselves here and now in the light of those historic words. This call to active engagement with the text is somewhat obscured by the unfortunate "This is the word of the Lord," which concludes the readings or the "This is the Gospel of the Lord," which concludes the gospel readings, and to which we are expected to respond "Thanks be to God" or "Praise to you, Lord Jesus Christ." The Latin original simply has *Verbum Domini* ("The Word of the Lord") in all three places, and it is far less oppressive. It is not a call to give assent to every line of the text, but to take on our responsibility as active agents and hearers of God's word, which includes the responsibility to face the often tragic limits of our own tradition, even our biblical tradition. By saying "Thanks be to God," we are not claiming divine origin for the notion that women should be subordinate to their husbands or that Jonah was literally swallowed by a whale, but affirming a willingness to grapple with the tradition through which we have heard God's voice, and within which we hope to continue to hear it, and hearing, follow it.

In common practice (it is encouraged by the official books), the gospel book is carried to the lectern with some solemnity, to the accompaniment of the Alleluia acclamation (or in penitential seasons, some other verse). The doing of this before the actual proclaiming of the text underscores the role of the people as active hearers and proclaimers. We are not simply responding to a given text, but owning up publicly to our responsibility to hear and proclaim the word, to be active agents of the gospel in the world.

On Sundays, the profession of faith (creed) follows the sermon. Since this entered the rite of mass nearly a thousand years

110

ago, the text has been that of the "Nicene Creed," the ecumenical creed of the churches of the East and West (though, in our usage, with certain Western additions). Liturgical scholars have often noted that it is somewhat superfluous in the eucharistic liturgy, since the eucharistic prayer itself constitutes our profession of faith. Accordingly, recent official directives allow a certain latitude in the choice of texts to be used here, and in some places you may find it omitted. The origin of the creed as a baptismal profession, however, may give it its own usefulness. We are not simply giving assent to a set of ideas, we are affirming a commitment to a way of life. In this, it has much the same function as the other acclamations, responses, and the Lord's Prayer.

The liturgy of the word concludes with the prayer of the faithful (or general intercessions). The General Instruction tells us,

> In the general intercessions or prayer of the faithful, the people exercise their priestly function by interceding for all mankind. It is appropriate that this prayer be included in all Masses celebrated with a congregation, so that intercessions may be made for the Church, for civil authorities, for those oppressed by various needs, for all mankind, and for the salvation of the world (No. 45).

In practice, there is often an artificial effort to relate these prayers to the readings of the day or the liturgical season, with the result that we end up praying mostly for ourselves, or at best for the pope, the sick of the parish, the dead, and ourselves. This is a tragic distortion of the prayer. Certainly, we may well pray here for the pope, the sick of the parish, the dead, and ourselves. But the point of the prayer is to call us outward to the wider world—to the needs of the larger church scattered throughout the world (How often are there prayers for the church in other countries, much less for our separated brothers and sisters in faith? How often do we pray for other parishes in the diocese? For the neighboring parish? For the Protestants across the street and the synagogue down the block?), to the needs of those in civil authority and those who work for justice, to the needs of the oppressed and deprived everywhere. The placement of the prayer of the faithful between the liturgy of the word and the liturgy of the eucharist is not accidental. It is a reminder that we are at eucharist, not simply for our comfort and consolation, but to take responsibility for the world in which we live. It is a reminder that we stand before the altar, not because we are called out of the world into a special sacred space, but because our business is to hallow the world, to make it a place where people find welcome, mercy, and a sense of their own dignity and responsibility. The collection will follow the prayer of the faithful, and rightly so. The gifts we are called to bring are our hearts prepared for the service of others.

Having explored the relationship of the eucharistic prayer to the whole of the Order of Mass, we are in a better position to understand why the laity have much more to say, or better, *sing* at the beginning of the prayer, in the introductory dialogue[4] and at the sanctus. The Christian calling is a call to joy, and the invitation to "Lift up your hearts" is a summation of Jesus' own invitation to those who would hear him. And if joy is the characteristic Christian emotion, the attitude that underlies it is one of gratitude, of coming to a recognition of ourselves as gifted, graced, blessed. The hallmark of Jesus' own prayer was gratitude. This gratitude is best summed up in the gospel by his naming of God as "father," and by his giving thanks at table— characteristics of the heart of his ministry. The invitation to "give thanks and praise to the Lord our God," and our response that it is right to do so, are, again, a summation of the whole Christian mission. In praying the Preface, the priest is simply giving voice to what we have already acknowledged as a heartfelt conviction.

If anything contrasts the present celebration of the eucharist with the mass of yesteryear, it is the acknowledgment of that call to joy. The medieval mass had its joyous tones, but in certain

[4] Priest: The Lord be with you.
People: And also with you.
Priest: Lift up your hearts.
People: We lift them up to the Lord.
Priest: Let us give thanks to the Lord, our God.
People: It is right to give him thanks and praise.

ways it more obviously constituted a call to awe. This is what invested it with a "sense of mystery" which many people now miss. That call to awe was capable of degenerating into a grim legalism or a querulous self-deprecation. If a cheery "I'm okay, you're okay" is the danger of present celebration, the danger of yesteryear was the assumption that none of us is okay, so we had better be careful about keeping the rules. One of the major reasons our working vocabulary of sacrifice has fallen into disuse is that too much of it reflected a grim distorting of a sense of holy awe into a fearful effort to keep a punishing God at a safe distance.

But the Christian gospel is a call to awe as much as it is a call to joy. Mary herself shuddered when the gospel announcement came to her, and the disciples at the resurrection tomb trembled. God is a holy God, and calls us to holiness. The holiness to which we are called, however, is not a holiness apart from life in this world. We are not called merely to find our own joy, but to help others find theirs, and ultimately to help the world to find its joy. As a people who have received mercy, we are called to go and do likewise.

The first movement of the eucharistic prayer culminates in the singing of the sanctus, which acknowledges that awesome holiness of God. It is unfortunate that it is so often merely recited or sung with tunes that do its keynote of awe less than justice. But it is not an awe that floats free from the gospel imperative to transform the world. By affirming that we join with "angels and archangels," the prayer is not inviting us into a never-never fantasy world. It is saying that our business is to join heaven and earth, to reveal God's glory. And, in the words of St. Irenaeus, one of the most venerable of the Fathers of the Church, the glory of God is humankind in all its wholeness.

Much of the dramatic impact of the eucharistic prayer, as a prayer which interprets the whole action of the eucharist, is diminished because of a widespread failure to implement one of the most important reforms in the rite of Mass—the restoration of the Breaking of the Bread as a significant moment. Coming as it does between the exchange of peace and the communion, the Breaking of the Bread should speak for the eucharist as being essentially a shared action, in which the whole point is to in-

113

terpret and affirm—through the spoken words of people and priest—our identification with the Christ who gave himself for others. That gesture utterly loses its point when it is not a breaking of a loaf to be shared, when it is only perceptible as a ceremony surrounding the "priest's host." We can scarcely appreciate the point of sharing a loaf unless it looks, tastes, and smells like bread to be shared.

If the Breaking of the Bread were a dramatic moment after the exchange of peace when the priest took the loaf and broke it in preparation for the sharing of holy communion, then we could more readily perceive ourselves as a people who stand before the Lord's table in both thanksgiving and acknowledgment of our need. We share others' tables, after all, both to honor them and to acknowledge our continued debt to their goodness. And the bread and cup of the Lord's table, like those of any good host, are food and drink shared. The relationship of the guests to one another is as critical as their relationship to the host. A genuine breaking of the bread (not just fraction of a wafer) would clarify both the priest's role as one of invitation and interpretation, and the people's role as one of action, for all our praying would culminate in that dramatic invitation to the moment of sharing.

Now that we have explored the relationship of the eucharistic prayer to the actions of the eucharistic liturgy as a whole, we are in a better position to perceive the eucharistic liturgy as the action of the assembly. Having been taught to perceive the mass after the fashion of a play to be watched, we have also tended to perceive the relationship between people and priest as one of "following" what the priest does. The tendency is to perceive the assembly as an appendage to the priest, and its actions and prayers simply as "responses" to his own. But we have identified the eucharist as essentially something that we all do. In outline, here is what we do.

We gather, identifying ourselves as
  a community that receives and
  gives God's mercy. (Introductory rites);

We name ourselves as a community of hearers
and proclaimers of the word, summing up
that role in the creed and in prayer for the
needs of humankind. (Liturgy of the word);

We "take" bread and wine, signs of the world of creation
and of human skill and striving, art and intelligence,
underscored by our presenting gifts of money.
(Preparation of the altar and gifts);

We give thanks and praise, identifying ourselves
with Christ who died and rose for our sake,
praying for the fulfillment of his life in
us by the power of the Holy Spirit, pledging
ourselves to live that life of Christ in the
world. (Eucharistic prayer);

We enact that commitment to share the life of Christ,
calling upon God as "Father," exchanging the peace,
and sharing together at the Lord's table. (Holy
Communion).

The actions and words of the priest are all at the service of those things we do. The relation of priest to people is not of actor to audience, nor even exactly of leader to led (our liturgical books *never* use a language that describes the priest as the "prayer leader"). The priest's role is to *invite* the assembly to what the assembly is there to do, and to *interpret* the meaning of what the assembly does. The traditional perception of the priest as having the essential task of consecrating the bread and wine supports rather than undercuts such a perception of the priestly role. That act is invitation and interpretation *par excellence*: we come to this table because it is the Lord's table; we stand before this altar to share the sacrifice of Jesus Christ. The priest's role is not to help us understand what the priest is doing, but to call us to an appreciation of what *we* are doing. Note that the priest does not begin by saying "The Lord be with me," but rather, "The Lord be with *you*." Likewise, before beginning the eucharistic prayer, the priest makes it clear that what he is about to do is done in our name: "Pray, my brothers and sisters, that *our* sacrifice may be acceptable to God the Father Almighty."

This should help to clarify the role of the priest's prayers, i.e., those which he utters in our name, normally somewhat longer than the short phrases we utter. There is a tendency to perceive these as the "main event," and it may underlie much of the hankering for more "poetic" prayers. But liturgical prayer (except for hymnody) is not poetry; it is dramatic prose. More to the point, the priest's prayers are *not* the "main event": they are commentary upon it, interpretation. The main event is what is *done*, and what is said or sung in acclamation by the whole assembly.[5] The prayers of the priest either precede or follow those main events, and they are to be understood as interpreting what we are about. Thus the "opening prayer" does not stand on its own: it is simply the priest's summation of what we have already prayed as a forgiving and forgiven community. Likewise, the great eucharistic prayer is commentary on the eucharistic action as a whole. It is the center and high point because of what *we* do, not because of what the priest says during that long moment. And what we do is expressed in our prayers and gestures through the whole mass, not simply at that moment that calls us simply to look and listen.

[5]By "sung," I do not refer here to hymns. In the context of the eucharistic liturgy, hymns are essentially ornamental. Only a puritan spirit would decry ornament, but let us not make more of them than they are. And like all ornaments, they can be a massive distraction from the real business for which we are gathered.

EPILOGUE

We began with the "loss of the sense of the sacred" in our world, a loss that is inevitable because the human experience of power is undergoing significant change. We explored the ways in which religious ritual empowers us and gives us a place to stand in the face of life's trials and ambiguities. And we explored the ways in which "traditional" Catholic ritual, i.e., the mass of the medieval church, worked with the images of God to empower people in the face of the world in which they lived. In the two final chapters, we explored the rearranging of the images of God in the rite of mass, and its potential for giving us a new sense of being an empowered people.

This is only a beginning, not an ending. The struggle to recover a sense of ourselves as the enfranchised people of God has only just begun. One finds the deepest sense of liturgical enfranchisement in fringe and splinter groups, and in churches not identified as "liturgical" churches. The ordinary experience of liturgical prayer remains an experience of being a spectator at a performance done by others. Our present religious horizon also includes elements that our present patterns of ritual prayer scarcely address at all. We live in a world that has become radically ecumenical. This manuscript is being typed within walking distance of access to groups that are impressive representatives of a variety of traditions of faith—Jewish, Black Muslim, Hindu, and witchcraft—all of them in a state of vigor and renewal.

Not every neighborhood is as diverse as Hyde Park, Chicago, but none of us can escape the living witness of other faiths as blessed and graced. The security of being "one, true church" and the confidence of praying "through Christ our Lord" is much more easily sustained when the religious others can be dismissed as adherents of a faith that is simply wrong or obsolete. We no longer have the luxury of that judgment, not only because it is now possible to perceive the others as blessed and graced, but because the world we live in leaves us experiencing our own tradition as "not enough," as in many ways failing us.

Yet this book is written in the belief that it is possible to pray, and indeed, to pray the Christian eucharist, in the midst of just such a world. The surest way to do that is to plumb the depth and breadth of our own tradition, not just as it has been mediated through the language and rituals of the past thousand years, but of the past five thousand. Theology names the event that the eucharist celebrates as the "paschal mystery," as an event of Christian passover. The Israel of God came to celebrate its passover as a memorial of the Exodus, of the passage from Egypt into the desert and the promised land, just as Christians came to celebrate the eucharist because of Christ's dying and rising, and named it as their paschal celebration. But Israel did not celebrate that history because it experienced itself as moving from triumph to triumph through history. It told and retold the story of the Exodus because, in a history of defeat and disappointment, exile and bondage, failure and the collapse of its ideals and institutions, it yet discovered itself to be a people in covenant with God, a people blessed and called even in the midst of all their trials. We have not understood the resurrection of Jesus very well if we perceive the New Testament witness as one of unremitting triumph. The disciples experienced the death of Jesus as a colossal letdown of all their hopes. The experience of resurrection was to find themselves called together as a forgiven and forgiving community, as created anew even out of the death of all their hope. The doing of the eucharist is a witness to ultimate power. But it is not power as we imagine or conceive it. To take bread and wine in thanksgiving is to affirm the sacredness of all the earth and the essential goodness of all human striving, in-

118

telligence, and skill. It is to name the world as the place where God is at work. To break bread together and partake from a common cup is to take a stand for the interconnectedness of the whole human enterprise. To do these things "in memory" of Jesus Christ is to say that these are the values worth living and dying for. And to do this as a community of sinners who identify themselves as the living presence of Christ for one another is to lay claim to mercy beyond all human terror and violence. And such is the kingdom of God that Jesus proclaimed.